**Understanding
World History**

The Late
Middle Ages

Adam Woog

**Bruno Leone
Series Consultant**

ReferencePoint
Press®

San Diego, CA

Once again, my thanks go to Stu Witmer for his advice and knowledge.

© 2012 ReferencePoint Press, Inc.
Printed in the United States

For more information, contact:
ReferencePoint Press, Inc.
PO Box 27779
San Diego, CA 92198
www.ReferencePointPress.com

LIBRARY OF CONGRESS CATALOGING-IN-PUBLICATION DATA

Woog, Adam, 1953–
  The late Middle Ages / by Adam Woog.
    p. cm. — (Understanding world history series)
  Includes bibliographical references and index.
  ISBN-13: 978-1-60152-188-0 (hardback)
  ISBN-10: 1-60152-188-X (hardback)
  1. Middle Ages. 2. Civilization, Medieval. 3. Europe—History—476–1492. 4. Feudalism—Europe—History. 5. Europe—Church history—600–1500. I. Title.
  D200.W66 2012
  940.1'9—dc22

                                                            2011001382

Contents

Foreword

When the Puritans first emigrated from England to America in 1630, they believed that their journey was blessed by a covenant between themselves and God. By the terms of that covenant they agreed to establish a community in the New World dedicated to what they believed was the true Christian faith. God, in turn, would reward their fidelity by making certain that they and their descendants would always experience his protection and enjoy material prosperity. Moreover, the Lord guaranteed that their land would be seen as a shining beacon—or in their words, a "city upon a hill"—which the rest of the world would view with admiration and respect. By embracing this notion that God could and would shower his favor and special blessings upon them, the Puritans were adopting the providential philosophy of history—meaning that history is the unfolding of a plan established or guided by a higher intelligence.

The concept of intercession by a divine power is only one of many explanations of the driving forces of world history. Historians and philosophers alike have subscribed to numerous other ideas. For example, the ancient Greeks and Romans argued that history is cyclical. Nations and civilizations, according to these ancients of the Western world, rise and fall in unpredictable cycles; the only certainty is that these cycles will persist throughout an endless future. The German historian Oswald Spengler (1880–1936) echoed the ancients to some degree in his controversial study *The Decline of the West*. Spengler asserted that all civilizations inevitably pass through stages comparable to the life span of a person: childhood, youth, adulthood, old age, and, eventually, death. As the title of his work implies, Western civilization is currently entering its final stage.

Joining those who see purpose and direction in history are thinkers who completely reject the idea of meaning or certainty. Rather, they reason that since there are far too many random and unseen factors at work on the earth, historians would be unwise to endorse historical predictability of any type. Warfare (both nuclear and conventional), plagues, earthquakes, tsunamis, meteor showers, and other catastrophic world-changing events have loomed large throughout history and prehistory. In his essay "A Free Man's Worship," philosopher and mathematician Bertrand Russell (1872–1970) supported this argument, which many refer to as the nihilist or chaos theory of history. According to Russell, history follows no preordained path. Rather, the earth itself and all life on earth resulted from, as Russell describes it, an "accidental collocation of atoms." Based on this premise, he pessimistically concluded that all human achievement will eventually be "buried beneath the debris of a universe in ruins."

Whether history does or does not have an underlying purpose, historians, journalists, and countless others have nonetheless left behind a record of human activity tracing back nearly 6,000 years. From the dawn of the great ancient Near Eastern civilizations of Mesopotamia and Egypt to the modern economic and military behemoths China and the United States, humanity's deeds and misdeeds have been and continue to be monitored and recorded. The distinguished British scholar Arnold Toynbee (1889–1975), in his widely acclaimed 12-volume work entitled *A Study of History*, studied 21 different civilizations that have passed through history's pages. He noted with certainty that others would follow.

In the final analysis, the academic and journalistic worlds mostly regard history as a record and explanation of past events. From a more practical perspective, history represents a sequence of building blocks—cultural, technological, military, and political—ready to be utilized and enhanced or maligned and perverted by the present. What that means is that all societies—whether advanced civilizations or preliterate tribal cultures—leave a legacy for succeeding generations to either embrace or disregard.

Recognizing the richness and fullness of history, the ReferencePoint Press Understanding World History series fosters an evaluation and interpretation of history and its influence on later generations. Each volume in the series approaches its subject chronologically and topically, with specific focus on nations, periods, or pivotal events. Primary and secondary source quotations are included, along with complete source notes and suggestions for further research.

Moreover, the series reflects the truism that the key to understanding the present frequently lies in the past. With that in mind, each series title concludes with a legacy chapter that highlights the bonds between past and present and, more important, demonstrates that world history is a continuum of peoples and ideas, sometimes hidden but there nonetheless, waiting to be discovered by those who choose to look.

Important Events of the Late Middle Ages

1096
The Crusades, a series of religious wars between Christians and Muslims, begins marking what many historians describe as the start of the late Middle Ages in Europe.

1075
The first of several major reform movements of the church begins, launched by a conflict between Pope Gregory VII and some of Europe's rulers over the power to appoint church officials to their clerical offices.

1000   1100   1200   1300

1086
A document that was probably the first census in Europe, the Domesday Book, is completed in England to provide information to the king on taxable property.

1108
The rule of Louis VI, a key figure in medieval France's influential Capetian dynasty, commences.

1215
King John of England signs the Magna Carta, a document in which the rights and privileges of his barons were recognized and guaranteed.

1272
The Eighth Crusade, the last of the major Crusades, ends.

1309

Clement V is elected and becomes the first of the Avignon popes, who move the headquarters of the church from Rome to the city of Avignon in France.

1378

The era of the antipopes begins—popes who challenge the right to rule of popes elected by church leaders in Rome; the resulting controversy is called the Western Schism.

1381

Wat Tyler's Rebellion, a rebellion by peasants against the royalty of England, takes place and becomes an important moment in the decline of the feudal system.

1429

Joan of Arc receives the first of her visions telling her to lead the French to victory in the Hundred Years' War.

1348

Bubonic plague, also known as the Black Death, strikes continental Europe; the plague would eventually kill millions of people worldwide.

1310 **1340** **1370** **1400** **1430**

1337

The Hundred Years' War begins—a series of conflicts between France and England over disputed lands in what is now France.

1417

A single pope is reestablished in Rome, ending the Western Schism.

Ca. 1450

The late Middle Ages come to an end.

1315

The Great Famine, the worst of several devastating famines, begins and goes on to kill millions across Europe and elsewhere.

Introduction

The Defining Characteristics of the Late Middle Ages

The era known as the late Middle Ages was a period of momentous and life-changing events. It altered forever the course of history in Europe and beyond. Wars, the rise of unified kingdoms, bloody battles among those nations, confrontations with the powerful Christian church, the loosening of a centuries-old system of economics and class—all of these and more carved the Continent into a new shape and foreshadowed equally sweeping changes to come.

No clear-cut markers define the beginning and end of the roughly five centuries that made up the late Middle Ages. Even today there is considerable debate among scholars about when this period began and ended. The period immediately before the late Middle Ages is often referred to as the early Middle Ages, an era that lasted roughly from the mid-400s to somewhere around the year 1000.

A date that is often cited as marking the beginning of the era that followed, the late Middle Ages, is 1096. That year marked the start of the first in a series of religious wars called the Crusades. These battles were between the Christian nations of Europe and the Islamic nations of the Middle East. The conflict between the forces of these two religions had begun in the seventh century and would continue, to varying degrees, to the present day.

The date marking the end of the late Middle Ages and the beginning of the next historical era is difficult to determine. Many historians point out that there is no single event that divides them cleanly. Nor did one simply end and the next begin. Instead there was a gradual overlap. However, many historians agree that the seeds of the next major period in European history, the Renaissance, were sown in the early 1300s, and that this new era was in full bloom by the mid-1500s.

The Rise of the Nation

Europe during the late Middle Ages experienced tremendous political, social, and economic changes. One of the most significant of these changes was a crucial shift in how Europe's governments took shape. During the last years of the early Middle Ages, the Continent was made up of a patchwork of small, localized states. Some of these realms were no bigger than a big city is today. A king or a member of the noble class exercised complete control over his realm.

As the late Middle Ages progressed, independent kingdoms gradually evolved. Some of them united with each other to form nations (or nation-states, as they are sometimes called) that were larger, stronger, and more organized. As in the localized states, a king typically had complete authority over each nation. The power of the newly formed nation-states grew as the power of the monarchies began to widen.

The Influence of the Church

Another notable change that took place during the late Middle Ages involved the church. During the early Middle Ages, or early medieval era, religion dominated virtually every part of European life. Historian J.M. Roberts comments, "The Church uniquely pervaded the whole fabric of society."[1] As a result of this widespread authority, the church wielded tremendous political and social power. Its influence was strong enough to affect the fortunes of entire nations.

To some extent, this situation continued into the late Middle Ages, as religion continued to have widespread control over European life. For example, the church was the driving force behind the most significant military event of the era, the Crusades. It also continued to wield strong political power; indeed, kings needed the support of church leaders to maintain their thrones.

However, sweeping changes in the relationship between church and state contributed to a gradual weakening of the former. In some ways the church remained as powerful as ever. In other ways, however, its power weakened during the late Middle Ages. In large part this was because of a series of scandals and divisions within the church that left it more vulnerable to dissent and criticism. One of these divisive factors came as the Crusades ended—more specifically, with the failure of the Crusades to achieve their main goal of bringing the Holy Land (a portion of the Middle East that is sacred to several religions) under Christian control. Another factor that had a negative impact on the church was seemingly ever-present corruption among church officials at all levels.

The Concept of Individual Rights

At the same time that the role of religion was transforming in the late Middle Ages, there was also a shift in the structure of European society and economics. This structure was a system known as feudalism. The feudal system was built on carefully separated social classes. At the top was royalty, or the noble class. Lords had their places below kings. In turn, peasants and serfs—the workers who toiled in the fields—were below the noble class.

A basic principle of feudalism was that these classes were bound together by close bonds of obligation and responsibility. People in a higher social class offered protection and the opportunity for livelihoods to people in lower classes. In exchange, the people in the lower classes promised loyalty and vowed to serve their lord.

However, during the late Middle Ages this system began to disintegrate. By the end of the era, it was nearly extinct. Europe was still based on an agricultural economy, as it had been since the earliest days. But the old system of strict, unchanging bonds of loyalty no longer dictated the Continent's economic and social life. In turn, this fostered the development of an important characteristic of the late Middle Ages: the rise in importance of the individual.

In earlier times individual people, even the most powerful, had in most cases few individual rights. During this period, however, the concept of individual human rights was very much on the rise. Medieval scholar Stu Witmer comments: "For me, a main theme of the period is the development of the individual. In Roman times there was little or no idea of the 'individual' but by the [end of the Middle Ages] there was no denying the individual as the most potent force in Western Europe."[2]

The Middle Class, Guilds, and Communes

Changes in economics and society gradually took the place of strict feudalism. Lords and peasants began to exercise their collective and individual rights. For example, the nobility started to demand the right to form councils that could vote on decisions of group importance, rather than deferring to absolute rule by a king. This gave many in the

Merchants show their wares to potential customers at a fifteenth-century market. The rise of the middle class, which consisted largely of merchants and other businesspeople, coincided with improved roads, increased trade, and the migration of rural people to cities in search of work.

upper classes more power and a greater say in governmental decision making—a step toward a modern, representative form of government.

Related to this was the birth and development of a new economic class: the middle class. This group was composed primarily of merchants and other businesspeople. The middle class rose at the same time that the economy bloomed during the late Middle Ages. This rise in the economy occurred, in part, because it became increasingly possible for traders to travel longer distances to sell or barter their goods. This created a demand for more goods such as tools, clothing, earthenware, and other commodities, which in turn led to bigger markets and cities where people gathered in search of work. The people who handled trade and other financial matters, and who were involved in the governing of cities, made up the newly evolving middle class.

As trade, urban life, and the middle class flourished, so did groups called guilds and communes. Guilds were organizations of craftspeople, artisans, and businesspeople that looked out for the mutual interests of their members. Similarly, communes were organizations that protected the interests of a city's inhabitants.

Guilds and communes were representative of still another change that took place during the late Middle Ages. This was a vast movement of people from rural areas to the cities. They sought to take advantage of the increased opportunities to create goods for trade.

A Time of Transformation

As all of these developments were taking place in Europe, changes were also occurring in other parts of the world. The most notable were in China, India, Japan, and the Near and Middle East. In China, for instance, the late Middle Ages marked a period of economic prosperity that included the establishment of a powerful navy and the development of gunpowder.

Japan also underwent important changes at this time. Beginning in the late twelfth century, it developed a feudal system that included, among other things, a complex and sophisticated government bureaucracy. Meanwhile mathematicians in India were making significant advances, including in the practical application of math in astronomy. And in the Middle East, by the tenth and eleventh centuries, technical advances in medicine had led to the invention of medical instruments such as scalpels, bone saws, forceps, and fine scissors for eye surgery.

In time, these and other revolutionary developments in areas such as technology and science filtered west, as settlers and traders of goods between Europe and Asia began opening lines of communication between the continents. These foreign innovations—along with developments within Europe itself—would have a profound influence on social, political, and economic life on the continent, altering the course of European history for centuries to come.

Chapter 1

What Events Led to the Late Middle Ages?

The characteristics of the late Middle Ages built on the developments of the era that preceded it. The early Middle Ages in Europe constituted a period of about 550 years, from roughly the mid-400s until around AD 1000. It saw the rise of three crucial elements in society and government. One was the dominance of politically distinct kingdoms where there had previously been a single large, organized empire. Another was the dominance of the Christian church. And the third was the development of feudalism.

The Roman Empire

While some scholars disagree, a commonly accepted date for the beginning of the early Middle Ages is 456. That year marked the end of the Western Roman Empire. The Western Roman Empire was a sprawling but highly organized realm that had dominated the European continent, as well as portions of the Middle East and North Africa, for hundreds of years before the start of the early Middle Ages. At its peak in the second century AD, the Roman Empire covered approximately 2.2 million square miles (5.7 million sq. km). Population estimates vary widely, from 65 million to 130 million, or somewhere between 20 and 40 percent of the world's inhabitants. The empire's success made it the greatest power in the world between the first and fifth centuries AD.

From the imperial city of Rome, the empire's rulers steadily pushed into new lands and expanded their holdings. They sent armies and administrators to every corner of their realm to protect it and battle against nations and tribes that resisted them. Organized and powerful, the Romans built bustling cities, defensive structures, and roughly 50,000 miles (80,000km) of roads throughout their empire. Their structures and roadways were so sturdy that remnants of them remain nearly intact 2,000 years later.

Few were able to fend off the mighty Roman legions. Prominent among those groups that resisted the invaders were fierce warrior tribes native to Ireland, Scotland, and Scandinavia. Those tribes that did come under Roman rule naturally began to assume the characteristics, customs, and manners of their new masters. Rome was able to introduce

Onlookers watch the procession of a triumphant Roman commander. The mighty Roman legions conquered many peoples but also introduced highly developed language, customs, arts, religion, and governmental structure to those cultures.

to these diverse groups of people its already highly developed language, customs, arts, and governmental structure.

In short, the Roman Empire was not merely a mighty military force and a solidly built, smoothly running administrative entity. It was perhaps the single most influential force in shaping the culture, religion, and structure of Europe in the Middle Ages. Notably, Rome introduced what became its official religion, Christianity, to the Continent, where it would eventually become the dominant religion.

Rome also had a profound effect on Europe's written and spoken language. This influence would continue throughout the Middle Ages and into modern times. Indeed, the written and spoken tongue of Rome, Latin, became the basis for five of the modern Continent's most widely spoken languages: French, Spanish, Romanian, Italian, and Portuguese. These tongues together are known by a name reflecting their origins—the Romance languages. (While it is not considered a Romance language, English also was influenced by Latin.)

The Empire Splits

However, the dominance of the Roman Empire was not to last. In 285, it divided into two parts. The western half of the realm encompassed roughly what is now western Europe. The eastern half, meanwhile, included Roman territory in parts of eastern Europe, North Africa, the Middle East, and what is now Turkey.

This split affected the future of Europe in several ways. One of the most important was that it caused a thinning-out and division of the empire's military resources. The frontiers of the realm became increasingly vulnerable to attacks from outside invaders. Its weakened state also created opportunities for various parts of the empire to rebel against Roman rule.

The hostile tribes of outsiders were called "barbarians" (from the Latin word for anyone living outside Roman territory). Among them were the Goths and Vandals, from what is now Germany; the Huns from what is now eastern Europe; the Lombards and Burgundians in southern Europe; and the Vikings from the Scandinavian regions. All of

Money

Money was an uncommon medium of economic exchange during the early Middle Ages. Most commerce was conducted through a barter system in which goods or services were traded. Coins were used, but because every kingdom made its own money, coin payment was confusing and cumbersome. Sometimes lords, towns, and even churches minted their own coins.

This situation persisted even after Charlemagne standardized money used throughout his kingdom in the late 700s. However, the situation changed as trade expanded, and by 1100 coins were increasingly important.

How much a coin was worth depended on what it was made from and its weight. Sometimes the value of a coin was changed through the simple act of cutting a bit off. However, if someone was caught clipping small pieces off and keeping the extra, the punishment was severe. (The process of cutting grooves around the edges of coins—milling—was begun in the fourteenth and fifteenth centuries in order to prevent people from scraping bits of metal from coins.)

The most common coin in the late Middle Ages was a silver penny with a Latin name, the denarius. Gold coins existed in western Europe, but these were left over from Roman times or new versions that came from the Byzantine or Islamic cultures. Then, in the mid-1200s, the city-state of Florence began minting gold coins, and other nations followed. By the 1400s a gold coin from Venice called the ducat was the most commonly used coin in Europe.

them were ferocious warriors with a reputation for ruthlessness. They made steady progress into Roman territory, taking control of much of the realm. Eventually the Western Roman Empire collapsed, while the eastern half (often called the Byzantine Empire) survived until 1453 when the Ottoman Turks successfully laid siege to the capital, Constantinople.

This collapse had a devastating effect on the governmental structure of the European continent. What had once been a highly organized and centralized realm quickly dissolved into chaos, fragmenting into many small political entities. These so-called petty kingdoms (a reference to their size) were disorganized and generally hostile toward one another. For the most part, the political situation in Europe would remain chaotic and disorganized throughout the early Middle Ages. (The short-lived empire of the emperor Charlemagne was the sole exception.)

It was not until the late Middle Ages that large, centrally ruled, and relatively unified nations began to form again in Europe. The fragmentation that characterized the early Middle Ages provided the political nucleus from which the succeeding period would evolve.

A Fragmented Society

Other aspects of European society were deeply affected by the legacy of the Roman Empire as well. These effects were felt all though the early Middle Ages and, in turn, had powerful repercussions for the events and trends of the late Middle Ages. Notably, there was the issue of religion.

In the fragmented condition of the early Middle Ages, the armies of Christian kings sought to convert nonbelievers to the Christian faith. The battle for Christianity proved successful, and it would remain the Continent's dominant religion—as well as a major force in society and politics—throughout the late Middle Ages (and into the modern world).

A third major development of the early Middle Ages that significantly affected the late Middle Ages was the rise of feudalism. The concept of feudalism was not new or confined to Europe, but during the early Middle Ages it became firmly entrenched there.

However, to a large degree it was able to flourish because of the fragmented state of the Continent's small kingdoms. Europe's economic system relied heavily on crops being harvested and distributed locally. In the absence of sturdy Roman roads, and of the security for travelers that the Roman military had once provided, extensive trade routes were typically nonexistent in the early Middle Ages.

The social aspects of feudalism were also able to grow and develop in the relatively fragmented and noncentralized state of the early Middle Ages. The rulers of various kingdoms, and the nobility under

The emperor Charlemagne, depicted as he receives foreign ambassadors, is considered by historians to be one of the greatest rulers of medieval Europe. Charlemagne influenced the course of events in Europe through his many reforms in education, economics, and culture.

them, were able to retain complete control over their lands and thus continued to dominate the peasants who worked the land. The fealty that existed among kings and the nobles helped provide the cohesion necessary to maintain relative order in early medieval society.

There was another, related element in medieval life that was affected by the fall of the Roman Empire. This was the failure of early medieval society to maintain and augment the cultural and intellectual achievements of ancient Rome. The Romans had always put an emphasis on literacy, scientific innovation, philosophical inquiry, and other enlightened aspects of civilization and culture. To a large degree, these were lost or ignored during the early Middle Ages, although they would be revived in the latter half of the era.

The Rule of Charlemagne

The one notable exception to the political, social, and cultural upheavals and chaos of the early Middle Ages was the emperor Charlemagne. Arguably the most significant figure of the early Middle Ages, Charlemagne began his long reign as king of the Franks in 768. The Franks were a Germanic tribe; theirs was one of a series of Germanic kingdoms, usually referred to by historians as "successor states," that ruled over the remnants of the Roman Empire in the west. The influence of the Frankish kings on western Europe was long lasting, but Charlemagne was probably the most influential of all. He was a born military leader and an extraordinary politician, and he is considered by virtually all historians to be one of the greatest rulers of medieval Europe. Charlemagne instituted many reforms, including the creation of a single monetary system. His reforms would have dramatic effects on the future of education, economics, and culture.

A notable example of this reform movement was the king's support for the creation of a standardized version of Latin. It served as a common, easily understood tongue that all of the empire's diverse cultures could use. This standard language remained the primary language among educated people across Europe for hundreds of years and was the cornerstone of what would later evolve into the Romance languages.

Charlemagne's Empire

NORSE

SWEDES

SCOTS DANES

Baltic Sea

North Sea

ANGLES AND SAXONS

WILZIANS

Aachen SAXONY

SORBS

SLAVS

AUSTRASIA

CZECHS

NORDGAU

MORAVIANS

Paris

BRITTANY

NEUSTRIA

BAVARIA

AVARS

CARINTHIA

BURGUNDY Venice

ALLEMANNIA

North Atlantic Ocean

CROATS

AQUITAINE

LOMBARDY

PAPAL STATES

BYZANTINE EMPIRE

SPOLETO

Rome

KINGDOM OF ASTURIUS

CORSICA

Barcelona

SARDINIA

SICILY

DUCHY OF BENEVENTO

MUSLIM TERRITORY

BALLEARIC ISLANDS

Mediterranean Sea

MUSLIM TERRITORY

	Charlemagne's empire in 771
	Areas added after 771
★	Capital

The system of government that Charlemagne developed also served as a direct predecessor to the developments of the late Middle Ages. Charlemagne's strong rule was by no means the only reason that the chaos of the early Middle Ages eventually grew into the relative stability of the late Middle Ages. Nonetheless, the ruler, and the increasingly unified kingdom that he led, provided a foundation for the changes that were to come.

The Size of Early Medieval Cities

European cities during the early Middle Ages were very small compared with those of the late Middle Ages. In fact, by the year 1000 there were still no large cities in most of western Europe. Venice was probably the most populous city in Europe during the early Middle Ages. Historians estimate it had a population of only about 8,000 to 12,000 toward the end of the period, primarily because its lucrative trade with Constantinople in the Byzantine Empire and Alexandria in Egypt attracted merchants looking for business and other people looking for work. J.M. Roberts comments that large cities such as Venice "were mainly to be found in Italy, where commercial relations with the outside world had been sporadically kept up even amid the upheavals of . . . invasions."

Things were very different in the Byzantine Empire, which enjoyed even greater prosperity than its trading partners to the west. Constantinople, for instance, had an estimated half million people at its peak during the reign of the Emperor Justinian in the mid-sixth century.

The situation in western Europe would change radically during the late Middle Ages, when economic changes brought a huge influx of people into urban centers. As Europe moved away from a strictly agricultural economy to one that also relied on trade and manufacturing, commercial centers like Paris, Venice, and London rapidly grew even bigger.

J.M. Roberts, *A History of Europe*. New York: Allen Lane/Penguin, 1996, p. 131.

One of his achievements was to succeed, to a high degree, in uniting a vast part of western and central Europe's successor states. A number of other kings had tried to do so in earlier centuries by waging war to absorb the regions around them. They were often unsuccessful, although they did succeed in laying the groundwork for future developments. Historian C. Warren Hollister notes: "During the centuries between the fall of the Roman Empire in the West and . . . the late eleventh century, the foundations were built on which Western civilization rose. Kingdoms emerged that would play dominant roles in the history of the modern world—England, Germany, France—and . . . that would define and vitalize Europe across the next millennium."[3]

Charlemagne came closest to this goal of creating a unified empire. The Frankish king did not unify all of Europe, but his realm was the most extensive Europe had seen since the Roman Empire of the second century. The heart of the Frankish kingdom was what are now the modern-day nations of France and Germany. At its peak, however, Charlemagne's empire covered a significantly larger part of the Continent. Indeed, it controlled most of western and central Europe with the exception of the Iberian Peninsula (modern-day Spain and Portugal).

Many historians consider Charlemagne's kingdom to be the predecessor of the coming era, the late Middle Ages. Historian Colin McEvedy comments: "Charlemagne's empire did not, of course, have much to do with the old Roman Empire; it didn't even have much resemblance to it geographically. However, the order he imposed on western Europe does represent a new base-line [starting point]."[4]

Charlemagne's Support of Religion

Yet another sweeping change that Charlemagne brought about—and that directly affected the late Middle Ages—concerned religion. Charlemagne was a devout Christian. He felt a moral obligation to spread the faith throughout his kingdom, and he worked tirelessly toward that end. The result was the conversion of much of Europe's population—including barbarian tribes—to Christianity during his reign. This shared religion, as with shared language and other aspects of society, did much to unite otherwise disparate elements within his empire.

Meanwhile Charlemagne's alliance with the pope, the supreme Christian leader, created a long-lasting union between religion and government—that is, between church and state. This alliance, in time, gave the church tremendous power and influence over medieval political history and daily life.

Charlemagne's successors were unable to maintain the unity and centralization he had forged, and in time his empire fractured and split into several smaller realms. It thus joined the rest of Europe's patchwork of small, political units. However, the governmental fragmentation would change as Europe entered the late Middle Ages and centralized kingdoms were once again gradually becoming the norm.

Chapter 2

Redefining Nations

The most crucial element in the political changes of western Europe during the late Middle Ages was the rise of centralized nations. These nations replaced the small and loosely allied kingdoms of earlier medieval times. Although their divisions and borders differed significantly from those of today, among the nations that were emerging during this period were France, Germany, Italy, and England.

With the notable exception of Charlemagne's empire, the Continent had for centuries remained a patchwork quilt of individual governments. Generally each of these kingdoms maintained its own laws, social structures, languages, traditions, money, and customs. Little was standardized, even within each state. For example, by one estimate the tiny region that is now the Netherlands had 700 legal systems during Charlemagne's time.

Military Strength

The small kingdoms of Europe slowly began to unite into larger, centralized kingdoms. The merging took place thanks to a number of factors. In some cases, for instance, small kingdoms joined forces to protect themselves from other realms. In other cases the mergers took place through violence—wars that led to one nation being annexed by another. This provided the framework for a steadily expanding civilization and a web of allied nations that would have been impossible to imagine in the early Middle Ages (which were sometimes erroneously known as the Dark Ages because the period lacked key elements of civilized life).

J.M. Roberts comments, "The eleventh century was to open a new era, one of revolution and adventure for which the centuries often misleadingly called the Dark Ages had provided the raw materials."[5]

Those nations that formed alliances recognized the advantages of unity. When allied as a single entity, nations wielded much greater power and influence than they did individually. One obvious advantage, for instance, was increased military strength. A powerful army was a crucial element in the ways a monarch achieved and retained his or her ability to govern, protect, and extend his or her realm. An example of this can be found in the long series of late Middle Ages clashes collectively called the Hundred Years' War. The two forces in this war, England and France, battled largely over who should rule portions of what is now France.

England and France both had the economic strength and political power to raise huge (and hugely expensive) military forces. Previously, the leaders of petty kingdoms had only been able to assemble ragtag armies for specific times of war. Occasionally, mercenaries were employed. Now, however, centralization gave unified nations the capability of replacing these limited, temporary military resources with larger, permanent armies. No longer did royalty have to cobble together temporary armies only in times of war. The monarch of a centralized country could require that the lords under him or her deliver certain numbers of soldiers every year to make up permanent armies. One such command, issued by William the Conqueror (King William I) of England to the senior member of a monastery, survives from the eleventh century. In part it reads: "Greeting. I command you to summon all those who are under your charge and jurisdiction to have armed before me by the week after Whitsunday [the seventh Sunday after Easter], at Clarendon all the knights which are due to me. And do you also come to me on that day and bring with you armed those five knights which you owe to me from your abbey."[6]

Bigger Government

In addition to greater military strength, the development of centralized nations allowed kings to create highly structured administrations. In

Joan of Arc

Joan of Arc (known in France as Jeanne d'Arc) was perhaps the most famous participant in the Hundred Years' War, and today she remains one of the greatest figures in French history. She has long been a national hero and the patron saint of France.

Joan was born about 1412 in what is now eastern France. She was an unlikely candidate for fame, being both a peasant and a woman at a time when neither was politically valued. Nonetheless, Joan became a brilliant military leader who did much to turn the tide of war in favor of the French.

While still a teenager, Joan began hearing "heavenly voices," and in 1429 the voices told her that her destiny was to save France. Despite her humble background, Joan's religious and patriotic devotion inflamed French troops to a fever pitch. Dressed as a soldier, Joan led her forces in a series of decisive victories, notably overcoming the English siege of the city of Orléans in north central France. (This victory earned Joan the respectful title of Maid of Orléans.)

Captured by the English in 1430, Joan was convicted of heresy and sorcery (in part because of the voices she heard). She was burned at the stake, the punishment usually accorded heretics. A quarter century later, the church retried her case and found her innocent. Centuries later, it officially declared her a saint.

this way a single leader could create and enforce regulations across his realm.

Maintaining a nationwide governmental structure required a large bureaucracy—that is, a system of regional administrators who were loyal to the king. This bureaucracy was responsible for a wide range of duties, including enforcing laws and holding criminal courts. An early example of a late Middle Ages monarch who established a significant bureaucracy was William the Conqueror. William sent a huge force of men across his entire country to assess the wealth of every region. The purpose of this was to determine how much tax should be paid to the central government.

One of the most important duties of regional administrators was the collection of taxes. Monarchs nearly always had a desperate need for taxes. This was largely because they needed money to maintain their lavish lifestyles and, in times of war, to deploy armies—which were ruinously expensive.

Shared Traits

The unity and stability of a nation depended on many other factors besides military strength and an efficient bureaucracy. For example, monarchs typically tried to foster a feeling of national pride and loyalty among their subjects. This was a good way to hold groups of people together and instill a feeling of common cause among them.

Among the attributes that a nation's people typically shared were customs, languages, physical characteristics, and traditional kinds of food. Perhaps the most important of these shared traits, however, was religion. Sharing a religion was a particularly powerful way for disparate groups to connect—and, if necessary, to unite against foreigners in times of war or invasion. Sometimes this national unity was just within one country; sometimes it served to ally a group of nations together against a common enemy.

The overall sense of national unity that arose in Europe during this period did not develop at the same time everywhere on the Continent. In some cases it did not develop at all. Nonetheless, it was a strong current running through the late Middle Ages. A good example of a people uniting because of national pride was in France during the series of conflicts with England called the Hundred Years' War. Like other emerging nations across the Continent, France was developing a strong sense of national pride. The French considered themselves an entity separate from others, just as the English did. The French armies and populace passionately united behind the figure of Joan of Arc during the final stages of this long war. The example of this young and charismatic leader helped France in the struggle, and she came to symbolize the kingdom's growing sense of national pride.

By the early fourteenth century, the citizens of a given European nation typically considered themselves different from people in other lands—not just from the next village or valley. Historian Roberts writes: "No medieval state was national in our sense. Nevertheless, by 1300 subjects of the kings of England and France could sometimes think of themselves as different from [outsiders] even if some Englishmen might still regard those who lived in the next village as virtually foreigners and even when not all Frenchmen were subjects of the king of France."[7]

French Kings in Hiding

As Europe's nations continued to develop, some emerged as more powerful and influential than others. One of these was France, which evolved from what had been the heart of Charlemagne's empire. France's development into a powerful, unified nation took several centuries.

By the ninth and tenth centuries, the once-mighty Frankish empire had declined under Charlemagne's descendants, some of whom were blatantly inept. Although officially it still had a monarch, in practice the region was divided into many small realms ruled by independent nobles. As a result, until the early twelfth century the French ruler controlled only a small part of what had been the Frankish kingdom. This was the Île-de-France, an area of land that surrounded and included Paris.

Many of the nobles who controlled regions beyond the Île-de-France were corrupt, oppressive, and quick to wage war. Furthermore, they had complete control over the kings of the Île-de-France. This was because they had the power to choose the rulers and naturally tended to pick ones weaker than themselves. Their control was so complete that the French monarchs often became virtual prisoners in their own domain. Historian Norman F. Cantor comments, "As close as ten miles

King Louis VI, depicted in a meeting with his subjects, guided France toward stability and prosperity during his reign. Through his actions he came to be seen by his subjects as a defender of religion, peasants, justice, and the independence of towns within his realm.

to the city [of Paris] the countryside was dominated by the castles of robber barons, and it is said that the . . . king feared to go outside the walls of his own city."[8]

Louis VI

This dire situation began to change during the reign of King Louis VI, who ruled from 1108 to 1137. Thanks in part to his charisma and personal bravery in battle, Louis (also known as Louis the Fat) raised a large army that helped him reclaim land that had once belonged to his line of rulers, the Capetian dynasty. He did so by securing roads leading from the countryside to Paris and by ruthlessly occupying or destroying the castles and lands of the individual warlords who opposed him. This effort took nearly a quarter of a century. In the process Louis actively sought the loyalty of ordinary French citizens, earning a reputation as a national hero and defender of religion, peasants, justice, and the independence of towns within his realm.

Overall, Louis regained firm control of his lands, and his successors continued this strong rule. They continued to curb the influence of the rebellious lords and expand Capetian power until the land under their control encompassed much of modern-day France. Furthermore, the extension of France's borders allowed trade to grow. In short, the Capetians ensured their nation's overall stability and prosperity. By the mid-1300s France was the most powerful nation in Europe.

England

France may have been the most powerful nation in Europe, but it was not the only one to establish itself during this period. England also developed during this time. The consolidation of England's smaller realms had begun in the early Middle Ages and was more or less complete by the tenth century. However, its strength was not felt to any great degree until the beginning of the late Middle Ages.

In large part a dramatic event in the mid-eleventh century was the reason. This was the Norman Conquest—an assault on England by an army from a region called Normandy (now in northwest France). After a decisive clash in 1066, called the Battle of Hastings, the Norman king William the Conqueror took control of England (which at the time covered much of the island that today also includes Scotland and Wales). William strengthened England's government, erected a number of fortresses and other buildings, and made other significant changes. Among these was the development of a superior naval force that in time made England into one of the driving forces in medieval politics.

Portugal

Still another important realm that represented centralization and growth during the late Middle Ages was Portugal. It became fully unified after the thirteenth century, in large part due to the conclusion of a long series of battles known as the Reconquista. During the Reconquista, Christian forces drove an Islamic group called the Moors from large sections of the Iberian Peninsula (the site of modern-day Portugal and Spain). The Moors were settlers who had occupied the region for centuries. No longer divided between Christians and Moors, Portugal emerged as a strong, separate, and centralized Christian nation.

Several factors contributed to Portugal's strength as a cohesive nation in the wake of the Reconquista. Its charismatic king, John I, earned the respect and confidence of the rulers of what had once been a collection of small domains. This made it possible for John to concentrate national power in his court. Furthermore, once the Moors were gone, the population of Portugal was again mostly homogeneous—that is, most of the people living there were of the same race, ethnic background, and religion, and most also spoke the same language. These common characteristics minimized the chances of civil strife and maximized feelings of national loyalty.

In addition, Portugal—located in the far southwest corner of the Iberian Peninsula—had always been geographically isolated. The only region it shared a border with was what is now Spain. This further bolstered the overall unity of its people. Furthermore, because of its isolation, Portugal's political structure was able to remain essentially intact after the Reconquista, even as the rest of Europe experienced periodic warfare and turmoil. And the Portuguese economy, based on fishing and trade by sea, remained robust and stable. In later times its wealth and long history of seafaring allowed Portugal to mount expeditions to faraway lands in Africa, the Far East, and South America.

The Rise of Diplomacy

Portugal continued to expand its borders, as did France, England, and other prominent nations. The monarchy well understood the importance of maintaining stable government within its borders, if only to minimize the possibility of rebellion. In addition to domestic affairs, however, foreign matters—especially relations with other nations—were carefully monitored.

English forces succumb to the Norman onslaught during the Battle of Hastings in 1066. The victorious Norman king, William the Conqueror, took control of England and then strengthened its government and developed a superior naval force.

Just as it does today, the success of a nation's foreign policy required a complex and intricate web of political connections. In some cases these relations were hostile—for example, when nations clashed over disputed territories—and sometimes led to war. In other cases relations among nations were cordial and peaceful.

One of the nonviolent ways of maintaining ties was through diplomacy, the use of negotiations to resolve issues of mutual concern. The concept of employing diplomats was a very old idea, one that had been in existence since the beginning of recorded history. However, its use reached new heights of sophistication and importance during the late Middle Ages.

King William's Rules of Conduct

William the Conqueror established certain rules for himself and his subjects after he completed his conquest of England. Among them were the following:

> First that above all things he wishes one God to be revered throughout his whole realm, one faith in Christ to be kept ever inviolate, and peace and security to be preserved between English and Normans.

> We decree also that every freeman shall affirm by oath and compact that he will be loyal to King William both within and without England, that he will preserve with him his lands and honor with all fidelity and defend him against his enemies.

> I will, moreover, that all the men I have brought with me, or who have come after me, shall be protected by my peace and shall dwell in quiet. . . .

> This also I command and will, that all shall have and hold the law of the king . . . in respect of their lands and all their possessions, with the addition of those decrees I have ordained for the welfare of the English people.

> I prohibit the sale of any man by another outside the country on pain of a fine to be paid in full to me.

> I also forbid that anyone shall be slain or hanged for any fault. . . . And this command shall not be violated under pain of a fine in full to me.

Quoted in Paul Halsall, ed., "Feudalism?," Internet Medieval Sourcebook, Fordham University History Department, March 21, 2007. www.fordham.edu.

The First Embassies

Previously, European countries had not typically maintained permanent diplomatic missions with each other. Instead rulers sent ambassadors to other lands to represent them only on special occasions, such as the signing of a treaty or a royal marriage. That practice changed, however, as nations grew larger and more politically active. The practice of establishing permanent embassies in other countries was a logical way to connect the Continent's increasingly forceful powers.

Beginning in the thirteenth century, full-time diplomatic missions were established. The first to test the system were five prosperous city-states. (City-states were cities that acted as their own independent nations.) Located in what is now Italy, these city-states were Milan, Venice, Florence, Naples, and the Papal States (a region controlled by the church).

The diplomatic missions they sent to each other allowed leaders to resolve disputes peacefully, make alliances and trade agreements more easily and efficiently, and otherwise maintain good relations with each other. The advantages of such ventures were quickly recognized elsewhere, and soon virtually all of the major European powers were exchanging permanent ambassadors.

Marriage

Diplomacy was not the only nonviolent way in which relations among nations were maintained. One method seems old-fashioned today, but at the time it was a crucial part of politics. This was the practice of arranging marriages between members of royal families. Arranged marriages had existed in earlier centuries, but during the late Middle Ages they reached new levels of importance in the political machinations of Europe.

Arranged marriages were intricate, strategically planned events that united royal families from different regions. There were several political advantages to an arranged marriage. For one thing, family ties were more likely to develop loyalty and peaceful relations. For instance, kings might be reluctant to go to war against each other if one was married to the other's sister or daughter. Furthermore, through inheritance, arranged marriages often provided legitimate reasons for acquiring new territories and expanding existing empires.

The royal family of the Habsburgs was especially shrewd in how it used arranged marriages to its advantage. The Habsburg empire was a formidable dominion, centered in what is now Austria, that had its origins in the early twelfth century and existed for hundreds of years after that. Jennifer Meagher of the Metropolitan Museum of Art in New York City notes that "the Habsburg dominion [expanded] dramatically over continental Europe not only through military conquest but also through carefully chosen marriage alliances."[9]

There are many examples of the Habsburg dynasty's use of arranged marriages. In fact, there were so many that they gave rise to an expression in Latin: *Bella gerant alii, tu felix Austria nube*—"Let others wage war: you, happy Austria, marry."[10] For example, Emperor Maximilian I, who ruled in the late 1400s, carefully arranged advantageous marriages for himself, his son Philip the Fair, and his grandson Ferdinand. Through these, the Habsburgs gained the territories of Burgundy (in what is now France), Spain, Bohemia (in what is now Germany), and Hungary without resorting to war.

A Century of War

However, the connections established through diplomacy or arranged marriages rarely solved every problem. As had been true since ancient times—and as is still true today—nations frequently went to war to resolve disputes and expand (or defend) their lands. In fact, during the late Middle Ages some violent conflict or other was underway somewhere in Europe at almost any given time.

One of the most significant of these wars was technically not a war at all. Rather, it was a series of clashes fought between 1337 and 1453 and collectively known as the Hundred Years' War. It is logical to think of them this way, as a single conflict, since they grew out of the same circumstance: a long-running dispute between England and France.

Arranged marriages reached new levels of importance in the political machinations of Europe's great powers during the late Middle Ages. Emperor Maximilian I (pictured) arranged many such unions to benefit the powerful Habsburg family.

The hostility began with a struggle for the throne of France following the death in 1328 of Charles IV, the last Capetian ruler. The reigning king of England, Edward III, proclaimed his right to inherit the French crown. He had some justification for this; his mother was the daughter of an earlier Capetian king, Philip IV. Furthermore, he had some claim to justice according to English law, which proclaimed that only firstborn male children could be rulers. Historian L. Kip Wheeler, writing about royal succession, notes, "All that matters in English law [of the time] is that the 'the blood of kings' runs in the firstborn male child's veins, even if that blood does not come directly through the father's [line]."[11]

Edward already controlled large regions of France, specifically parts of Normandy and all of Aquitaine. This was a legacy of the connection between England and France that William the Conqueror had created centuries earlier.

The Long War Continues

As might be expected, the noble families of France vehemently denied Edward's claim. To them, it was clear that the English king was interested only in furthering his own interests, not those of France. Their justification for refusing Edward was a French law concerning the line of succession, which made Edward ineligible. The French nobility offered the crown instead to Philip's distant relative, Philip of Valois. In response Edward invaded France, seized Calais (a major port), and won a series of subsequent battles.

However, the English forces were not able to definitively defeat the French, and the fighting continued sporadically for decades. Each of the individual wars was inconclusive, and the adversaries took turns claiming victory. The last battle in this drawn-out conflict took place at Castillon in France in 1453. Historians generally consider the outcome to be a victory for the French, who were able to force the English armies out of most of their territory and maintain their nation's independence.

The Rise of Islam

The Hundred Years' War was an example of a conflict that pitted two European nations against each other. But another series of clashes—even more prolonged than the one between France and England—united the governments of Europe in a common cause. This was the threat of invasion by Islamic warriors from the Middle East. These Muslim forces were intent on occupying Christian lands and converting the inhabitants to Islam. The aggression was by no means one-sided; Christian armies had invaded Muslim territory as well for the same purposes.

The two religions had been at odds ever since the death of Islam's founder, the Prophet Muhammad, in the early 600s. With amazing speed, Islamic forces had risen up and occupied vast regions in what are now central Asia, the Middle East, North Africa, and Europe. Colin McEvedy comments, "Within twenty years of the Prophet's death, the Arabs had created an empire to rival Rome's."[12] The intensity of the Islamic-Christian conflict waxed and waned over the centuries. Nonetheless, throughout the late Middle Ages it remained a constant presence around the Mediterranean world and, in some cases, beyond.

Other Sources of Turmoil

Conflicts involving Islamic armies and conflicts among the nations of Europe were by no means the only sources of turmoil on the Continent during this period. During the late Middle Ages, one of the most powerful entities in Europe, the church, also faced new challenges. Since the church's influence crossed the borders of European nations, it was often embraced by those nations' rulers—and just as often it clashed with them.

Chapter 3

Religion and the Church

By the beginning of the late Middle Ages, the church had become such a powerful force that it often could affect the political fortunes of entire nations. However, as European nations grew more unified and powerful, their leaders became more assured and thus were increasingly able to assert their own political power. As a result, the church's influence and control suffered, and it increasingly came in conflict with the rulers of various nations.

This was symbolized by an eleventh-century event called the Investiture Controversy. This was a disagreement over who could appoint high church officials to their positions and who could invest them with the symbols and power of their office. Should it be the church or civil authorities? The question was important, in part, because these offices could be sold for large profits to appointees who were loyal to one side or the other. The right to make appointments was therefore an obvious advantage. Pope Gregory VII decreed in 1075 that only the church had the power of investiture. This was part of a broader position that asserted the pope's power above any worldly king.

The most prominent ruler on the opposing side was Henry IV, the king of Germany (which included part of Italy at the time). Furious at Gregory, Henry withdrew his support from the papacy. Gregory retaliated by excommunicating the ruler—that is, banishing him from the church, an act that automatically barred a person from reaching heaven. Gregory declared: "I deprive King Henry . . . who has rebelled against [God's] church with unheard-of audacity, of the government over the whole kingdom of Germany and Italy, and I release all Christian men from the allegiance which they have sworn or may swear to him, and I forbid anyone to serve him as king."[13]

Canossa

This power struggle between church and state pleased Henry's political opponents in Germany. They heeded the pope's words and declared themselves independent of Henry's kingdom. Faced with a rebellion, Henry was forced to yield to Gregory's wishes regarding the investiture question and, by extension, the political power of the church.

In the winter of 1077 the king made a long trek over the Alps to the northern Italian city of Canossa, to meet with the religious leader. Gregory humiliated Henry by making him stand as a penitent sinner

Henry IV, king of Germany, kneels outside in bitter weather awaiting an audience with Pope Gregory VII. The pope's humiliation of Henry took place during a power struggle between the church and the king. Henry later exacted revenge when he deposed Gregory and installed a pope of his own.

barefoot in bitter weather until the pope granted him an audience. McEvedy comments, "One of the enduring images of medieval history is the Emperor Henry in the shift [clothing] of a penitent [someone repenting his sins], waiting for the Pope's forgiveness."[14]

Gregory did take Henry back into the church. Once Henry returned home, however, the king wasted no time in taking revenge for Gregory's humiliating actions. He organized a large army, crushed his enemies in Germany, and marched on Rome. Then he deposed Gregory and installed a pope of his own.

Despite the presence of a sympathetic pope, however, the Investiture Controversy dragged on until 1122. That year, at a conference called the Concordat of Worms (which took place in Worms, Germany), a complex agreement was reached in which the church agreed to share the rights of investiture with secular authorities.

The Investiture Controversy thus became a powerful symbol of one of the most important trends of the late Middle Ages, as the nations in Europe continued to become solidly organized and enjoy the power that came with it. Nonetheless, the church remained a major force during the late Middle Ages. It continued to act as a crucial part of Europe's spiritual, social, and political life.

For one thing, the church was an economic powerhouse. It was the largest landholder and employer on the Continent. Historians estimate that about 20 percent of the population had direct connections to the church as priests, monks, nuns, or other clergy. Thousands more were laborers and administrators for church property. Because of this and other factors, many historians suggest, religion remained the single most important characteristic of the era. J.M. Roberts comments, "To understand medieval Europe, the place to begin is the Church."[15]

The Crusades

As the Investiture Controversy dragged on, the church began to pursue a new goal, that of conquering or retrieving land under Muslim rule. The goal was twofold. The pope knew that a holy war—a crusade—

Saint Francis of Assisi

The setbacks the church experienced during the late Middle Ages led to a number of attempts to reform it. These movements were not always successful, but they laid the groundwork for the Reformation, the revolution that ripped the church in two in the sixteenth century.

Of course, not all clergy were in need of reform. The church was full of honorable men and women who provided positive illustrations of the church's power to do good works. Among the most notable of these were the many devoted Christians of the late Middle Ages who were later elevated to sainthood by the church.

Perhaps the most famous example of these saints was Saint Francis of Assisi. Francis was an Italian monk who lived from about 1182 to 1226. He devoted himself to a life of solitude, prayer, poverty, and aid to the poor and sick. The Franciscans, a religious order tracing its origin to Saint Francis, is well known even today. The order focused (as it still does) on maintaining vows of poverty, simplicity, devotion to God, and aid to the sick and poor. According to historian C. Warren Hollister, Francis was "perhaps the most widely admired figure of the Middle Ages."

C. Warren Hollister, *Medieval Europe: A Short History*. Boston: McGraw-Hill, 1998, p. 219.

would extend Christianity's physical boundaries into the sacred Holy Land. By showing that the church had the power to raise a huge army from a number of different countries, a crusade had the added advantage of bolstering the papacy's power.

A war to achieve these objectives required the cooperation of both church and state. The partnership would strengthen ties between nations and the church. It would also unite all of Christianity in a common cause.

These aims resulted in one of the defining events of the late Middle Ages. This was the Crusades, the series of wars fought over the course of nearly two centuries (1096 to 1272). Most of the Crusades were fought to control the Holy Land known as Palestine, sacred to Christians, Muslims, and Jews. The crown jewel of this prize was the city of Jerusalem, which by the early eleventh century had been under Muslim rule for nearly 400 years. At the same time, some crusaders fought to free land from Muslim rule in other regions, notably the Iberian Peninsula.

The Pope's Call to Arms

The Crusades began in 1096 with a call to arms from the reigning pope, Urban II. He was in part inspired by a request from the emperor of the Byzantine Empire, a Christian, who needed help in fending off invading Turkish Muslims. This original goal soon expanded to include an assault on the Holy Land.

One incentive that the pope used to spur interest in the proposed holy war was the promise of a valuable spiritual reward. Urban announced that "soldiers of the church," as they became known, would be guaranteed forgiveness of their sins, as well as a place in heaven, whether they survived or died in battle. He also promised papal protection of property and family while the crusaders were away.

Urban further stated that anyone—even criminals—were welcome to join the battle. He proclaimed: "Let those who have for a long time been robbers, now become knights. Let those who have been fighting against their brothers and relatives now fight in a proper way against the barbarians. . . . As soon as winter is over and spring comes, let them eagerly set out on the way with God as their guide."[16]

Pope Urban II calls on loyal soldiers of the church to embark on a crusade to the Holy Land. Thousands answered the call to join the First Crusade.

Answering the Call

This call to arms proved exceptionally appealing. In addition to the promise of spiritual reward and the chance for glory, potential holy warriors were also motivated by greed. Urban held out to them the promise of riches—vast treasure and land in what he proclaimed was an abundantly fertile region. Norman F. Cantor writes, "He offered . . . the prospect of carving out kingdoms in Palestine, 'a land flowing with milk and honey.'"[17]

The idea of a large-scale, far-off campaign against a formidable enemy attracted tens of thousands of men who accepted the pope's challenge. Each took a sacred vow to fight—to the death, if necessary—for Christianity. Europe's aristocracy was generally also eager to take part in the war and lent both moral and financial support.

The numbers are difficult to determine, but one estimate suggests that about 30,000 soldiers took part in the First Crusade, which lasted from 1096 to 1099. Although modest by today's standards, this was an immense army for the time. These men, sometimes accompanied by their families, came from all levels of society, from the nobility to the peasant class. Kings, however, were conspicuously absent from the First Crusade.

As they left Europe, the crusaders eagerly marched to war. One observer who witnessed knights on their way east wrote that they "sang warlike songs so joyously that they seemed to look upon the approaching battle as if it were a sport."[18]

The First Crusade

The soldiers met in the Byzantine capital of Constantinople in the summer of 1096, proceeded to Jerusalem, and immediately entered into battle. As might be expected, they met with fierce opposition. Islamic forces defending the city were joined by Jews living in the region, who were outraged by ongoing massacres and persecutions of their people in various parts of Europe. According to one estimate, in the first six months of the First Crusade, approximately 10,000 Jews were murdered in Europe.

The Knights Templar

When Christians established themselves in the Holy Land after the First Crusade, a number of elite military-religious organizations formed to give the Christian settlers aid and protection. Among them was the Knights Templar.

Like the other orders, the elite soldiers of the Knights Templar were eager for battle. But they had other tasks as well. They protected the supply route to Christian territories. They helped expand a lucrative trade route farther east into Asia. And they protected travelers who were making pilgrimages to the Holy Land.

The Knights Templar shrewdly set up an early form of banking. They held money for traveling pilgrims in special accounts, which the travelers redeemed at the other ends of their journeys to and from the Holy Land. This protected the pilgrims by making them less susceptible to bandits.

The commission from each of these transactions, combined with donations from the Christian faithful and any treasure claimed in battle, made the Knights Templar fabulously wealthy. The church augmented this financial gain by guaranteeing that the order was answerable to no authority and paid no taxes.

The Knights Templar used their profits to buy land and construct fortresses all across Europe and the Middle East. They also owned a fleet of ships and invested in businesses such as manufacturing, importing, and exporting. Because these financial interests were spread across a number of countries, some historians consider the Knights Templar to be the first multinational corporation.

The ongoing persecution of Jews was ordered by rulers or lords in many parts of Europe, and the church generally turned a blind eye to it or, in some cases, even sanctioned it.

Jerusalem's defenders at first held the Christians at bay. However, in 1099 the crusaders finally succeeded in entering Jerusalem, where they killed all the surviving Jews and Muslims. They also sacked the city, destroying buildings and confiscating treasure. A Christian eyewitness wrote, "If you had been there you would have seen our feet colored to our ankles with the blood of the slain. . . . None of them were left alive; neither women nor children were spared."[19]

After securing Jerusalem, the Europeans then spread into the surrounding territory and founded new states. In some ways the crusades that followed the first one were essentially missions to resupply and sustain these newly Christian-held lands in the face of ongoing Muslim attacks.

Some crusaders remained behind in these new states. Others returned home and received heroes' welcomes. They brought with them, as expected, great treasure, including gems and gold. They also brought back precious relics—that is, artifacts believed to be tokens of Christianity, such as the bones of saints or slivers of the true cross, which according to Christianity was the cross on which Jesus died. All in all, despite some heavy losses, the First Crusade was a victory for the Christians.

Routes of the First Crusade

The Crusades Continue

Meanwhile Muslim forces were regrouping. When in 1144 they succeeded in retaking the strategic region of Edessa (in modern-day Turkey), the church issued a call for a new religious campaign. This was the Second Crusade, which lasted from 1147 to 1149. This time the Muslims prevailed, and the Christian forces failed to retain most of the territory in the Holy Land that they had previously seized. Historians generally view the Second Crusade as a disaster for the Christian forces. On the other hand, the crusaders maintained their hold on Jerusalem.

Forty years later, the great Muslim warrior-ruler Saladin recaptured Jerusalem after nearly a century of Christian rule. He left Christian churches and shrines more or less intact and spared many of his enemies. This was not entirely a merciful act, however; Saladin exchanged his hostages for a fortune in ransom.

Germany, France, and England sent significant forces on the Third Crusade in an attempt to oust Saladin from Jerusalem. That crusade lasted from 1189 to 1192. However, the Christian leaders disagreed on a number of issues, and this lack of unity led to failure. The Europeans did have one partial success, however. They negotiated a treaty with Saladin that would allow unarmed Christians to enter Jerusalem as pilgrims.

The crusades that followed were progressively smaller, more disorganized, and less successful for Christians. The Eighth Crusade, which ended in 1272, is considered the final major campaign. One reason for the lack of success in these later crusades was that European nations were unwilling to commit large forces. The rulers of these nations also refused to continue fighting a faraway battle, since they were often preoccupied with conflicts closer to home.

A New Crisis

With the exception of the First Crusade, the holy wars had not achieved much for the church, which faced more difficulties in the years to come. Only a few decades after the final major crusade, the church encountered several interrelated and debilitating crises.

One of these involved increasing conflicts with European royalty. For centuries the church had maintained its role in controlling elements of politics by allying itself with a succession of compliant kings. Now, however, as national political power grew, the rulers of European countries were increasingly confident in their ability to challenge the papacy.

The conflict came to a head late in the thirteenth century. Pope Boniface VIII issued a statement that upheld the right of the church to wield absolute power over all nations and their rulers, stating that total allegiance to Rome was the only means of salvation. The pope, he declared, was the supreme authority—an "emperor sent from heaven [who] can do whatever God can do."[20]

France Versus the Pope

But Philip IV of France, Boniface's chief rival, was a shrewd adversary, and he devised a way to increase his control over Rome. Philip transferred the administration of France's legal work from the hands of church officials (where it had been for years) to his own lawyers and bureaucrats. He also began heavily taxing the church, a practice previously unheard-of. Boniface retaliated by issuing a declaration, known as a papal bull, forbidding taxation without his approval and threatening to excommunicate any monarch who defied him. Philip then prohibited all transfers of money from France to the papal center in Rome. These funds were crucial to the operation of the church. Boniface was forced to amend his statement, asserting that taxation of the church would be acceptable, but only during an emergency.

Tension continued to mount, and at one point Philip unsuccessfully attempted to have Boniface taken prisoner. In 1309, with Philip's backing, a Frenchman was elected pope. This was Clement V, who was, not surprisingly, sympathetic to the French king. Unwilling to endure the hostile atmosphere that his enemies in Rome created, Clement moved the papal court from Rome to Avignon, a city in what is now southeastern France. Six more popes would lead the church while quartered in Avignon, all of them loyal to the French monarch.

The great Muslim warrior Saladin (pictured) recaptured Jerusalem from Christian forces after the Second Crusade. He left many churches and shrines intact and ransomed many of his enemies rather than killing them.

The Western Schism

The court of the pope did not return to Rome until 1378, but this hardly put an end to the church's problems. In fact, an even more serious period of trouble was about to begin. Roberts comments, "When the papacy returned to Rome . . . it [faced] the greatest scandal in the history of the Church."[21]

This scandal was the Western Schism. (A schism is a serious split.) It was touched off in 1378, when Urban VI became the new pope. He was an erratic leader—suspicious, overbearing, and hot-tempered. Colin McEvedy comments, "Urban's failings were considerable. The cardinals in particular found it difficult to deal with a Pope who was constantly threatening them with physical violence."[22]

Church leaders withdrew their support of Urban and tried to replace him with Clement VII, the first in a series of so-called antipopes (a term used to describe unofficial popes who challenged popes who had been officially elected). Though Clement VII was elected, Urban refused to give up his position. Two rival popes now presided over opposing factions and their struggle became a battle among Europe's national powers, most of whom backed either Clement or Urban. For example, France supported the Avignon papacy, while England supported Rome—a situation that only fueled the longtime animosity between these two nations. The debate, and sometimes open warfare, dragged on for 50 years.

A number of solutions were proposed to resolve this embarrassing, baffling, and sometimes bloody situation. But for years complex church laws and doctrines blocked any proposed solutions. In 1409 a council of church elders was convened to find a solution. However, the council did nothing more than elect another pope, Alexander V, thus succeeding only in compounding the problem. Three rivals now claimed the papal throne, continuing until Alexander's death in 1410, when he was possibly poisoned by a rival.

In 1414 yet another meeting of church leaders was convened to resolve the strange state of affairs. After several more years of maneuvering, the council obtained the resignation of the reigning pope, Gregory XII of Rome, and of the antipope, John XXIII of Avignon. It was agreed that a single person, Martin V, would assume the papacy in Rome, which he did in 1417. Although more antipopes appeared later, the long and bitter Western Schism was essentially over.

The Church's Influence on Education

Despite the Western Schism and other difficulties, the church continued to retain its power over several areas of life. One of the most important of these was education. During the early Middle Ages, the church had more or less completely controlled every aspect of education. Notably, it had established schools for reading and writing, but these had generally been only for members of the clergy. Church officials needed to be literate so that they could read the Bible aloud. The vast majority of people—including many members of royalty—had never learned to read or write.

Then, in the years overlapping the early and late Middle Ages, the church expanded its role in education. Specifically, it became involved in the formation of universities—independent schools devoted to teaching, study, debate, and research. Higher education of this kind was a revolutionary development, one that had not been seen in Europe since the end of the Roman Empire.

The First Universities

Europe's first universities were in Bologna, Italy, and Paris, France. By the mid-1200s major institutions had also been founded in other cities in Western Europe including Toulouse, France; Salamanca, Spain; and Coimbra, Portugal.

The phenomenon continued to spread. By 1400 there were more than 50 universities across Europe. The most prestigious of these was the University of Paris. The French monarchs enthusiastically supported it, in part for the general benefit of the nation and in part because it was a source of well-educated, dedicated employees of the court and the huge national bureaucracy.

The church, expanding its original stand on learning, also supported the development of universities. In part this was because being well educated was considered an important advantage for anyone who wanted to work in the church.

The church had a significant amount of influence over subject matter and teaching style at these schools. However, over the years universities began putting more emphasis on nonreligious, or secular, education. That is, the subjects that were studied in universities were not necessarily seen only through the lens of religion.

Art and Literature

University cities, as might be expected, were prominent centers for innovation and experimentation of all sorts. Law, literature, art, architecture, medicine, technology, and music grew and developed explosively in university cities during the late Middle Ages.

Much of this creative effort was supported or directly sponsored by the church. Not surprisingly, the subject matter was almost exclusively religious. Metalwork, sculpture, painting, illuminated manuscripts, stained glass, and textiles were just some of the art forms brought to fruition during this period. Many of these works were created by unknown artists. Exceptions are the Italians Fra Angelico and Giotto and the Dutchman Jan van Eyck, three of the period's most brilliant painters. Often, works of art from this period mixed religious devotion with secular interests.

Science

The church also supported many aspects of scientific research during this era, and the study of science was a frequent occupation for monks. A major incentive for this was the creation of practical methods for furthering religious knowledge. For example, an understanding of astronomy was needed to predict the date of Easter. Similarly, medical knowledge aided those communities of monks devoted to helping the sick and injured. (Of course, knowledge in this field was still severely limited, and by today's standards medieval medicine was primitive and barbaric.)

The most prominent church figure connected to scientific inquiry during the late Middle Ages was Roger Bacon, a Franciscan monk of the 1200s. In particular he sought to revive the spirit of study that had existed in ancient Rome and Greece. As a result, Bacon made significant advances in a wide variety of fields, including optics, astronomy, and anatomy. (He was also keenly interested in alchemy, which was largely concerned with chemical experiments designed for purposes such as turning lead into gold.)

Not all scientific and technological research was directly connected to religion. For example, the era also saw the creation of secular and thoroughly practical inventions such as mechanical clocks, eyeglasses, crossbows, cannons, and spinning wheels. Furthermore, there were significant advances in mathematics and other intellectual fields. (Many inventions and innovations—among them gunpowder, paper, the modern form of writing numbers, and compasses—originated in China or the Islamic world before making their way to Europe.)

The Church's Power Wanes

Notwithstanding its role in supporting education, the arts, and science, overall the church's power declined somewhat during the late Middle Ages. Its influence on daily life had once been unquestioned and virtually complete, and in the twelfth and thirteenth centuries it had enjoyed the height of its power as a political force. However, by the early fourteenth century the institution's influence was waning.

There were several reasons behind this. One was widespread dismay over the results of the Crusades, the costly and bloody wars that had nonetheless failed to regain the Holy Land. The disruptive scandals and confusions of the Avignon papacy and the Western Schism served to further weaken the church's authority. Even widespread outbreaks of disease (such as the bubonic plague or "Black Death" in 1348) played a role, since the power of prayer was unable to stop them. Thus, by the early 1500s the papacy was less of a pervasive force than it had been in earlier centuries.

Still, the church's influence was not, by any means, gone. For one thing, it was still a major economic force, and kings had to deal with the church on a financial level. And, of course, it continued to wield social power, since Christianity remained the religion of virtually all of Europe. But the church was not the only powerful force in society during the late Middle Ages. Another cornerstone of life was the economic and social structure called feudalism.

Chapter 4 🌐

Feudalism, the Medieval Economy, and Society

During the early Middle Ages, feudalism evolved and eventually matured into a functional political system of government. But the system remained a cornerstone of European society well into the late medieval era. And, like Christianity, it saturated virtually every aspect of life.

Feudalism's role in the medieval economy was based on the fact that Europe was overwhelmingly rural. The system was thus intimately tied to the land and agriculture. By extension, the control of property was the primary source of wealth. For all practical purposes, land equaled wealth. A good harvest proved profitable for the lord of the manor; a poor harvest could mean starvation for those living on the manor.

Feudalism

Typically, the king owned all the land in his nation. He then awarded parts of it to the lords below him but retained the right to take it back if certain obligations such as military service were not met by the lord receiving the land. This land could legally be further divided among lesser lords and knights. Landlords—as the name implies, lords who controlled a given tract of land—were absolute authorities within their realms. They administered justice, gathered taxes, managed farms, and controlled many aspects of their workers' lives. They could even decide who could marry whom.

The lands that the nobility managed were called fiefs. A fief's profits came from crops, fees for grazing and fishing rights, timber, livestock, and game. Indirectly, a fief produced other sources of revenue such as rent to use the lord's mill, a license to collect tolls on a road, or even permission to mint money.

Feudalism was clearly unfair in many ways to many people. However, seen strictly as a political and economic system, feudalism worked fairly well. It established and maintained a well-organized means of bringing in crops, managing land, levying armies, collecting taxes, and performing other actions to keep the system functioning. And everyone, including the king, had duties and obligations for which they were legally responsible.

In some ways the social hierarchy of the Middle Ages can be seen as an extension of religious thought of the time. According to medieval Christianity, a person's duty was to stay where God willed—a clear parallel to feudalism. In other words, a human could not choose where he or she stood in society. One's station in life was accepted as being predetermined by God. Historian Jacques Le Goff comments, "Rising in society was a sign of pride; demotion was a shameful sin. The organization of society that God had ordained was to be respected, and it was based on the principle of hierarchy."[23]

The Social Ladder

But there was another basic component of feudalism beyond the economic. The system also depended on a sharply defined social hierarchy—that is, on layers of classes. One's position in a given class was hereditary and rarely changed. At the top were members of the royal class. Below them were the nobility: lords and lesser lords. Peasants were a further step down in status. Many peasants worked directly for their lords, receiving a relatively small portion of the fief's crops and livestock. Other peasants were tenant farmers, who were part of a more complicated arrangement in which they leased farmland and shared their harvest with their lord.

Peasants of the late medieval period work the land. Many peasants worked directly for their lords and, in return, received a small portion of crops and livestock from the lord's holdings.

Although their lives were humble, peasants were not the lowest of the social classes. Below them were the serfs, who did the most menial work. Serfs were not technically slaves, but they were bound so intimately to their masters, with so little chance of breaking away, that the appearance of servitude was always there.

Classes were bound together by a complex set of contracts. These ties connected peasant to lord, and lord to king, in mutually beneficial ways. Feudalism thus was a unifying system linking the entire social spectrum into a single chain and relying on ties of personal honor and loyalty.

Fealty

Generally, these links were based on contracts between individuals. Someone in one social class offered protection, support, and reward to someone in a lower class. In exchange, the person in the lower class promised loyalty, an agreement to work, and a portion of the land's profits. This worked both ways. In other words, lords offered financial support and protection from danger to peasants. At the same time, the lords were beholden to their king for the same benefits.

Obligation and responsibility were the cornerstones of feudal contracts. When someone in a given class swore loyalty to a lord, that person made a promise called an oath of fealty. For instance, a king might grant a fief, title, or position of authority to a lord. In return, the lord pledged his fealty. He swore allegiance to the monarch, which typically included promises to assemble an army in wartime and to deliver a percentage of any profits from the fief. Peasants swore somewhat similar oaths to their lords.

Safer Travel

Another crucial aspect of the economy in the late Middle Ages was a boom in trade and commerce. This boom was created by several factors. One of these was the improvement of roads. The Romans had built sturdy highways crisscrossing the Continent. During the early Middle Ages, with no central authority to maintain them, these roads had fallen into disuse and disrepair. Now, however, centrally administered nations could improve them, which in turn supported economic growth.

Improved roads meant an improved economy for reasons beyond the obvious one of easier travel. For one thing, law enforcement (a function also made possible by centralized governments) meant that people could travel the highways with a higher degree of safety. This was especially important for traders who carried valuable goods. Historian Will Durant, commenting on the dangers that traders faced, wrote, "Merchants were adventurers, explorers, knights of the caravan, armed with daggers and bribes, ready for highwaymen, pirates, and a thousand tribulations."[24]

In conjunction with the improved road system was another phenomenon that further helped reduce danger. This was the trade fair. These fairs were organized at least annually in regions along the old Roman routes. For instance, one of the largest fairs was in the French province of Champagne, which held six a year.

Fairs were popular with merchants because they only needed to travel as far as the fair, not to the ultimate destinations of their goods. This, of course, cut down on time, expense, effort, and danger. The cities where fairs were held benefited in many ways but especially financially. They could charge merchants for services such as the use of booths, as well as for food and lodging.

New Luxuries

Safer roads and trade fairs were major factors in the economic boom of the late Middle Ages. In contrast to the stagnation of the early Middle Ages, by the early 1200s the overall European economy had risen to new heights. While much of this activity was within a given country or even smaller regions, international trade was also brisk. For example, eastern Europe, the Continent's main source of gold, grew wealthy trading with western Europe. Other regions concentrated on manufacturing and trading commodities such as glass, leather, iron tools, and ships.

As might be expected, royalty and landed nobles benefited the most from increased trade. They were, after all, the ones who could best afford to buy goods. C. Warren Hollister comments, "Money and commerce made new luxuries available to the landed aristocracy: pepper, ginger, and cinnamon for baronial kitchens; finer and more colorful clothing; jewelry; fur coats for the cold winters (and to impress the less fortunate); and—for the castle—carpets, wall hangings, and more elaborate furniture."[25]

Cloth was an especially important trade commodity. English farmers raised sheep that yielded high-quality wool, which merchants sold elsewhere—particularly in what today is referred to as the Low Countries (Netherlands, Belgium, and Luxembourg). These countries then turned the raw wool into high-quality garments and sold them elsewhere. As a result, the cloth-manufacturing cities of the Low Countries, notably Ghent and Bruges, became significant commercial hubs. Colin McEvedy writes that these cities "rivaled London and Paris, the emerging political centres of the region."[26]

What the Magna Carta Said

Some of the Magna Carta's clauses are irrelevant today. However, others outline principles of law that remain fundamental to modern society. The "Great Charter" represents a milestone in the acceptance of certain individual rights and outlined the basic ideas behind representative government—specifically of England's constitutional monarchy, which combined royalty with a parliament of representatives.

These passages from a modern translation of the Magna Carta illustrate its relevance to current thinking about individual liberties. (As used here, "we" refers to King John; this is a traditional form of royal speech.)

> The keeper of the land of . . . an heir who is under age is only to take reasonable receipts from the heir's land and reasonable customs and reasonable services, and this without destruction or waste of men or things. And if we assign custody of any such land to a sheriff or to anyone else who should answer to us for the issues, and such a person should commit destruction or waste, we will take recompense from him. . . .

> No sheriff or bailiff of us or of anyone else is to take anyone's horses or carts to make carriage, unless he renders the payment customarily due . . . nor will we or our bailiffs or anyone else take someone else's timber for a castle or any other of our business save by the will of he to whom the timber belongs.

Source: Featured documents, Magna Carta. National Archives and Records Administration, www.archives.gov.

The Hanseatic League

Better roads were not the only way to ship goods. Sea routes were also important. Along the Mediterranean, for instance, coastal cities such as Venice, Genoa, and Pisa (all in today's Italy) prospered by expanding their shipping capabilities.

Meanwhile a vast sea-trading organization formed in northern Europe. This was the Hanseatic League, which at its peak in the late fourteenth century had 170 member cities. At the height of its operation, the league controlled virtually all commerce among coastal regions from the Baltic Sea to the North Sea. Its members traded goods such as furs, grain, wine, livestock, honey, wool, cloth, metal ore, fish, and timber.

As the league grew, it established its own enforcement agency for protection against pirates and other threats. It also developed its own decision-making groups and mutual aid societies. Furthermore, the league founded schools to train ship pilots and built its own lighthouses and warehouses. On occasion, the organization even raised an army to protect its interests. For example, it waged war against Denmark between 1361 and 1370, forcing the Danish king to grant more favorable trading conditions.

Guilds

As the Hanseatic League and other aspects of Europe's expanding commerce flourished, another sign of the times appeared. This was the development of guilds, which were organizations of craftspeople and businesspeople. Craft guilds existed for artisans such as cobblers, woodworkers, stonecutters, brewers, and bakers. Merchant guilds, as the name implies, were for traders and other dealers in commodities.

As depicted by a fifteenth-century artist, the late Middle Ages boasted a variety of artisans including cobblers, woodworkers, stonecutters, brewers, and bakers. Many of these craftspeople formed guilds to provide assistance and protection to members.

Like members of today's labor unions, members paid annual dues to a guild. In return, the guilds provided a variety of services. For example, they supported the families of sick or injured members. A guild also promised protection for property and people, supported new business ventures, and negotiated disputes.

Guilds had other roles as well. They monitored business practices, the treatment of apprentices, and quality standards. Furthermore, guilds connected their members socially. For example, they might sponsor festivals in honor of their patron saint. These saints were said to protect particular organizations. For example, Saint Augustine was the patron saint of brewers, while jewelers came under the protection of Saint Eligius.

Communes and the Middle Class

As guilds developed, Europe saw the refinement of a related institution: the city commune. A few communes had existed in the early Middle Ages, but during the late Middle Ages they became much more sophisticated. Communes provided protection and other services for all of a city's inhabitants in much the same way that guilds aided their members.

Some communes grew so powerful that they could challenge lords who imposed burdensome taxes and other unfair practices. In some cases cities were able to free themselves entirely from these local lords. Some urban centers achieved this through large payments. Others fought for it.

Royalty frequently supported cities in these fights for freedom. There were several reasons for this. For one thing, an urban center that was no longer controlled by local lords sent its taxes directly to the monarch's treasury. Furthermore, people in free cities were often more loyal to the monarch than to their lord. This helped the king control rebellious lords.

Along with the rise of guilds and an increase in commerce came the development of a new social stratum: the middle class. This class, primarily urban, occupied a place between nobles and peasants. Broadly speaking, members of the middle class were people who engaged in commerce and the creation of products. The middle class typically also included city leaders and administrators.

Paying Homage and Pledging Fealty

This passage (in modernized English) describes a ceremony held in 1127 in which knights paid homage (respect) and pledged fealty to their lord, the count of Flanders. (Flanders is now part of Belgium.)

> On Thursday the seventh of April, homages were again made to the count being completed in the following order of faith and security.
>
> First they did their homage thus. The count asked if he was willing to become completely his man, and the other replied, "I am willing"; and with clasped hands, surrounded by the hands of the count, they were bound together by a kiss.
>
> Secondly, he who had done homage gave his fealty to the representative of the count in these words, "I promise on my faith that I will in future be faithful to count William, and will observe my homage to him completely against all persons in good faith and without deceit," and thirdly, he took his oath to this upon the relics of the saints.
>
> Afterward, with a little rod which the count held in his hand, he gave investitures to [appointed] all who by this agreement had given their security and homage and accompanying oath.

Quoted in Paul Halsall, ed., "Feudalism?," Internet Medieval Sourcebook, Fordham University History Department, March 21, 2007. www.fordham.edu.

Changes in Population

Large and well-organized guilds and communes, as well as the middle class, developed in parallel with another significant social change: a movement in Europe's population from the country to the city, with people migrating in search of better work. It was only natural that they would join guilds and otherwise become involved in the life of their cities. The influx of people led to enormous growth in urban centers. For instance, the once small city of Paris swelled to an estimated population of 300,000 by about 1475—a huge number by fifteenth-century standards.

There were also other factors in Europe's population changes during this time. The number of people living in Europe had dropped steeply in the early Middle Ages, in large part because of a series of plagues and famines. However, around the year 1000 these numbers began to rise quickly. Figures are sketchy, but one estimate puts the total number of people in Europe in the late 700s at about 30 million. By about 1100 that figure had jumped to an estimated 70 million to 80 million. One reason for this dramatic change is that there were relatively few natural disasters, such as plagues and famines, during the period. This created a baby boom effect: More people survived long enough to have multiple children and create a new and larger generation.

Improvements in agriculture also helped. Among these were the introduction of two- and three-field crop rotation, better water mills, windmills, and farming tools such as improved plows and scythes for cutting grain. These produced better harvests and allowed farmers to expand their usable land. Increased food production, in turn, sustained life further. Hollister comments, "To feed the millions of new mouths, the process of land clearing [and planting] accelerated."[27]

Famine

However, this boom in population did not last. Early in the fourteenth century, Europe's population growth dropped to essentially zero. One reason for this was the Great Famine of 1315–1317. The Great Famine was caused by two years of cold, near-constant rain that left crops rotting in fields all across northern Europe. (The Continent's southern regions were largely spared because two mountain ranges, the Alps and the Pyrenees, kept the bad weather from moving south.)

Exact figures are uncertain, but it is known that millions perished during this time. One estimate has it that 10 to 25 percent of the residents in some regions died. As conditions worsened, the famine's victims became increasingly desperate. What little bread was available became too expensive for all but the wealthiest who made up only about 5 percent of the population. Children were abandoned to fend for themselves. Crime skyrocketed as people resorted to any means available to find food, and there were even widespread reports of cannibalism.

The Black Death

But the devastation of the Great Famine paled in comparison to an even crueler disaster later in the same century: a plague called the Black Death. It was by far the most terrifying disease outbreak of the Middle Ages—and one of the worst in world history.

The Black Death first hit Europe between 1348 and 1350. The epidemic wiped out as much as half the population of the Continent—about 100 million people, according to some estimates. Crowded cities, where the chances of infection multiplied, were hit especially hard. In Paris alone, a reported 800 people died every day during the worst of the plague years. Some towns and villages lost up to 75 percent of their population. With so many dead, bodies were often left to rot in the streets.

Disease had always been a danger in the Middle Ages, due in large part to the high level of ignorance of the human body, illness, and medicine as well as to poor nutrition and the absence of hygiene. (According to some sources, baths were considered bad for the health, and people typically took only a few every year.) As a result of these conditions, the average life span was only about 35 years—and plague obviously lowered that life span dramatically.

Although historians disagree on exactly what the Black Death was, it likely was a bacterial infection caused by a bacillus, *Pasturella pestis*. Although it is commonly referred to as bubonic plague, two other varieties also existed: pneumonic and septicemic plagues. Bubonic plague began with fever and excruciatingly painful swellings in the groin and armpits. Black and purple spots then appeared on the body, and death arrived within days. The mortality rate for the two other varieties of plague was even higher than that of the bubonic plague. The Italian author Giovanni Boccaccio, who lived through the epidemic, wrote that those struck by the plague "ate lunch with their friends and dinner with their ancestors in paradise."[28]

Labor Shortages

In addition to the obvious tragedy of millions of deaths, the famine and plague of the fourteenth century had far-reaching economic consequences. One aspect of this was that widespread death created a steep decline in commerce and trade, because there was less demand for goods. For example, exports from the winemaking region of Bordeaux (now part of France) at the end of the fourteenth century were roughly one-tenth of what they had been at its start.

There was also a severe shortage of laborers for farm and manufacturing work. To bring in their crops, landlords were forced to hire anyone who had survived—including people with no farm experience. The same was true for workshops in cities. Any survivors who could work, meanwhile, were able to demand incentives such as more food, extra pay, and better living conditions.

As a result, overall the standard of living for workers rose sharply. There were a few exceptions, however. For example, in 1351 King Edward III of England declared that prices and wages would be frozen at pre-plague levels. Edward also banned peasants from leaving farms and, in an effort to increase the labor pool, required beggars to find work.

Meanwhile, although agriculture remained important, the shift to urban populations was creating an increasing movement away from the land-based economy that feudalism relied on. A different focus for the economy emerged. The manufacture of goods for trade, rather than locally grown and distributed crops, was increasingly the basis for economic growth.

The Beginning of the End of Feudalism

The peasant class realized that the labor shortage had radically changed the division of power among social strata, both in the country and the

Residents of Florence, Italy, lie sick and dying in the streets during an outbreak of bubonic plague, also known as the Black Death. Historians say the epidemic, which first struck Europe in the mid-1300s, killed about 100 million people.

city. Peasants quickly grasped the fact that they now had a significant degree of control over their working lives. In other words, long-exploited peasants were discovering that they had the power to upset the established system. Le Goff comments, "When necessary, medieval man had learned how to become a rebel."[29]

A number of strikes and revolts resulted from this growing awareness. One example was the Peasants' Revolt (also called Wat Tyler's Rebellion after one of its leaders). This uprising took place in England in 1381. Demands to put an end to a crushing tax inspired a mob estimated at 100,000 to storm London and its surrounding villages.

The throng demolished the lavish Savoy Palace and killed the archbishop of Canterbury and other officials. It also nearly succeeded in reaching King Richard II before he hid in the Tower of London. The king did not have the forces necessary to stop the rebellion, so he confronted the protestors personally. Richard promised that he would enact reforms, and the mob dispersed. Within weeks, however, the king reversed his promises and hanged the leaders of the revolt. Without them, the rebel forces weakened, and Richard was able to crush them.

The Magna Carta

Similar protests were occurring across Europe. Like Wat Tyler's Rebellion, not all were successful, but collectively they sent a strong message: The peasantry would no longer accept the restrictions of times past.

The rising tide of peasant revolt was related to another important development in society during this period. It concerned a growing confidence among lords in demanding individual rights, as well as a greater say in governing and lawmaking. This at first only affected the noble class, although in time it would profoundly affect other classes as well.

This shift was symbolized by a revolutionary document that was drawn up and signed in 1215. It was called the Magna Carta. (The term means "great charter.") This document was not the first or the last of its kind, but it was by far the most influential—in fact, it was one of the most far-reaching documents in medieval history.

The oppressive policies of England's King John I triggered its creation. John's abuse of royal powers—in particular a demand for crushing taxes—inspired 40 lords to refuse to pledge their continued loyalty to him. Instead they united their forces and marched on London. Reluctantly, John met with the rebels, who presented him with the document they had drawn up. The king, lacking the forces to overcome the rebel army, was forced to affix his royal seal to it. In return, the lords agreed to renew their oaths of fealty to John.

A Rich Legacy

It would have been impossible at the time to predict the future influence of the Magna Carta. Using the example of the document's birthplace, historian Chris Given-Wilson writes: "In 1215 no one would have known what the word 'parliament' [a legislature] meant. . . . By the early fourteenth century, however, parliament had already established its central role in English political life."[30]

The new changes did not take effect immediately. As soon as John put his seal on the Magna Carta, he announced that it was invalid because he had been forced "by violence and fear . . . to accept an agreement which is not only shameful and demeaning but also illegal and unjust."[31]

Not surprisingly, open war broke out. Louis, the crown prince of France (later Louis VIII), agreed to join the rebels. John was forced to flee, and Louis led an army to London, where he was proclaimed king. However, following John's death in 1216, the lords withdrew their allegiance to Louis, convinced that he had his own plans to keep the lords at bay so he could retain power himself.

Instead they supported John's young son, Henry III, whose reign was being administered by royal advisers until he came of age. After a year and a half, Louis gave up his claim to England's throne and returned to France in frustration. When Henry became an adult and personally took power, he modified the Magna Carta but kept its essential spirit intact, and he honored its terms.

Similar documents soon appeared in other nations. Within a century, the spirit of the Magna Carta had spread throughout Europe, particularly its assertion that royalty had an obligation to share decision making with a body of elected representatives. J.M. Roberts comments, "By the end of the thirteenth century few countries had not experienced some summoning of representatives."[32] France, for instance, had the Estates-General while England had its Parliament.

The assertion of rights represented by the Magna Carta, the decline of feudalism, and the rise of the middle class continued to affect European economics and society. Together with other factors that arose during this period, they form a rich legacy—much of which has survived into the present day.

Chapter 5

What Is the Legacy of the Late Middle Ages?

The late Middle Ages left a remarkable legacy for future years. The events of the era led to sweeping changes in European civilization. These changes included lasting reforms in government, religion, the economy, and individual rights. Indeed, the entire Middle Ages significantly influenced European history throughout the modern era. Historian Geoffrey Barraclough asserts that the medieval period, in fact, marked the true beginnings of a recognizable European culture. He writes, "Medieval history, in its broadest connotation, is the story of . . . the rise of a distinctive European civilization."[33]

Furthermore, many of these developments affected the world far beyond the European continent. These developments are still having a profound impact on life today around the globe. Historian Paul Marie Viollet comments, "The roots of our modern society lie deep in [the Middle Ages]. What we are, we are in large measure because of the Middle Ages. The Middle Ages live in us; they are alive all around us."[34]

Political Relationships

One of the most far-reaching legacies of the late Middle Ages was the rise of nations. Small, relatively weak and chaotic kingdoms coalesced during this period into larger, stronger, and more centralized nations. This process had begun earlier, but in the late Middle Ages it came together in a far more permanent and systematic way. During the Renaissance, which followed the late Middle Ages, many European nations grew even more powerful because of these changes. For example, England's centralization gave it the wealth and resources to develop a military fleet that prevailed over all others. This development led directly to other developments in later centuries. Notably, England's naval power allowed it to fend off invaders, explore new lands, and establish colonies and trading ports throughout the globe. In later centuries this resulted in England becoming arguably the most influential country in the world.

The stirrings of diplomacy in relations between nations of the late Middle Ages grew into formal relationships as time progressed. Strategic partnerships in times of war existed before the late Middle Ages, but the formation of permanent diplomatic missions during the late medieval era was a new development—and its legacy can be seen right up to the present day. Specifically, the medieval establishment of embassies—or the closing of them—led to a powerful political tool that is still in use. Embassies remain symbols of friendship between nations and practical methods by which they can conduct affairs with each other.

Economics and Trade

The late Middle Ages also left a crucial legacy for modern economies. For example, a medieval king who ruled over a centralized nation had the ability to create a single form of money that could be used throughout his realm, rather than the confusing array of money that individual lords used within their own smaller territories. A king also had the ability (and need) to create a bureaucratic system that collected taxes and administered them in central locations.

The legacy of these developments can be found across the modern world. Many of the world's local, state, and national governments collect taxes from their citizens to fund infrastructure and essential services. And standardized currency has long been the rule in most countries; Europeans have gone even further by adopting a standard-

Monuments to God

Until the twelfth century most buildings of any size that belonged to the church were monasteries or convents designed to house communities of monks and nuns. Later developments led to the creation of huge, ornate cathedrals, especially in northern France and England. These soaring structures are still some of the great glories of European art. J.M. Roberts comments:

> They were both offerings to God and an essential part of the instrumentation [establishment] of evangelism and education on earth. About their huge naves and aisles moved processions of relics and the crowds of pilgrims who had come to see them, sometimes from hundreds of miles away.
>
> Their windows were filled with the images [of the religion] which was the core of European culture; their façades [outer faces] were covered with . . . representations of the fate awaiting just and unjust. . . . Its full impact on the imagination of medieval Europeans is hard to grasp unless we remember how much greater was the contrast its splendour presented to the reality of everyday life than any imaginable today. And that it had no competition.

J.M. Roberts, *A History of Europe*. New York: Allen Lane/Penguin, 1996, p. 165.

ized currency that crosses national borders. That currency is known today as the euro.

Modern trade and commerce, both within nations and internationally, also have roots in the late medieval era. For example, currency reform led to increasingly sophisticated ways of buying and selling goods.

The increased level of commerce during this period had a crucial effect on the development of a new social stratum, the middle class (which was later to develop into the leaders of modern industry). At the same time, the late Middle Ages' system of improved trade and the related rise of the middle class were direct predecessors of the economic system of capitalism, which eventually became the economic system for many nations.

Guilds and Communes

A related legacy of the late Middle Ages and one that is still an important part of the world economy was the guilds and communes. Guilds were the predecessors of modern labor unions that protect the interests of workers around the world. Examples include organizations such as the Teamsters in the United States and the many French unions gathered under the umbrella of that nation's Fédération des Bourses du Travail (General Confederation of Labor).

Medieval guilds established a number of business practices that have lasted into modern times. One of these was the concept of copyright. Copyright law concerns the belief that credit for creations or innovations by individuals should be recognized, and that those individuals should be compensated for them. In other words, the person who is responsible for the creation of something is entitled to exclusive rights to its manufacture and profits.

For example, medieval bakers would slash the tops of their bread loaves in certain ways. These distinctive marks proved that the bread came from a particular individual. The mark was also a form of quality assurance. It was a guarantee that the product came from a reputable member of the bakers' guild and that it met standards set by the guild. A similar example of copyright protection in the modern world can be seen in the creation of computer software. The inventor of a program can copyright that program. He or she is then the only person who has the right to mass-produce commercial versions of it or assign another the right to produce it.

President Barack Obama delivers his second State of the Union address to a joint session of Congress in 2011. Democracy and representative government existed before the late Middle Ages, most famously in ancient Greece, but were revived and refined during the late medieval period.

Representative Government

The decline of feudalism and the blurring of the sharp distinctions that separated social classes created still other important legacies for the future. These are the related concepts of democracy and representative government.

Democracy is a system that allows citizens to actively participate in government. It does this by letting them vote on decisions that concern them. Democratic governments stand in sharp contrast to other forms of rule, such as oligarchies (rule by a select few) and monarchies (rule by a king or queen). Because citizens are allowed to take part in the decision-making process, democracy creates a greater degree of equality.

A political system that is related to democracy is representative government. In this system, citizens vote for representatives to stand in for them when decisions are made and laws are passed. Today, representative government is recognized by much of the world. Notable examples of these are the US Congress and Senate, Germany's Bundestag and Bundesrat, and Great Britain's Parliament.

Of course, democracy was not the dominant form of government in Europe during the late Middle Ages. In almost all cases, only royalty had the power to make decisions and laws. There were a few exceptions, however. For example, Iceland held an annual assembly of both citizens and chosen representatives. This council, the Althing, was founded in the eleventh century. It continues today, in a modified form, as the world's oldest representative body still in existence.

The concepts of democracy and representative government were not invented in the late Middle Ages. They date far back in history and were used in several ancient cultures, the most famous being Greece. But it was the revival and refinement of Greek democracy during the late Middle Ages that gave the medieval period one of its greatest legacies.

Religion

Religion was a crucial part of life in the late Middle Ages, and it would continue to be so in future eras. However, the challenges to the church's dominance during this period had a profound effect on future society. The tests that the church endured during the late Middle Ages resulted in a widespread shift in its power in political affairs, in the role of religion in daily life, and in the rights of individuals to practice their faith as they wished. In turn, these reappraisals resulted in a series of shattering events whose effects can still be seen today.

These events, in large part, grew out of charges of widespread corruption within the church. Although the church's priests, monks, bishops, and nuns were sworn to chastity (that is, they were not to be sexually active), many of them simply ignored this vow. While some affairs were conducted in private, a number of high church officials openly had mistresses and fathered and raised children. Among the clergy who flagrantly violated their vows were a number of popes, including Innocent VIII and Alexander VI.

Challenges to the power of the church during the late Middle Ages altered its traditional dominance of daily life and political affairs. Eventually dissent from within split the church in two during the Reformation. One of the leaders of the Reformation, Martin Luther, translates a Bible in this illustration.

The Domesday Book

As reading and writing became more commonplace among the upper classes in the late Middle Ages, written documents were preserved—unlike previous centuries, when oral tradition was the primary means of maintaining important records. Being able to keep written records made it possible to maintain an efficient government. Clearly, the advent of written records has been key to this and many other aspects of life ever since.

An example of an early written record for administrative purposes was the Domesday Book. This was a massive study ordered by King William I of England (William the Conqueror) shortly after his Norman troops took possession of the island. (The origin of its name is not clear. It may refer to the biblical Judgment Day, or "doomsday." In other words, it is a judgment—the final word.)

Completed in 1086, the Domesday Book was a survey of much of England and parts of Wales for administrative and tax purposes. The king needed detailed records so that his newly established bureaucracy could work efficiently. As might be expected, this was especially important when the information helped William collect taxes. The king therefore ordered that inspectors be sent into every part of England to note the size, ownership, and assets of each parcel of land in his realm.

Another charge that was widely made against the church had to do with financial corruption. Many officials, especially those who had high positions within the church hierarchy, abused their power and enjoyed lavish, extravagant lives. The most brazen of them lived in splendid houses, ate the finest food, and indulged in such luxuries as jewel-encrusted clothing. In order to support themselves, naturally, these religious officials needed equally extravagant incomes.

To do so, they frequently turned to corrupt practices. An example of this concerned the widespread practice among the faithful of making pilgrimages to sacred sites, churches, and cathedrals that held important religious relics. Those who had authority over these holy places charged pilgrims exorbitant admission prices. Members of the church hierarchy also sometimes sold religious relics—or forgeries of relics—to wealthy monarchs and others who desired them.

The most profitable of these corrupt financial practices—as well as the most controversial—concerned the selling of indulgences. An indulgence was an official religious ruling that a person was absolved of all sins and guaranteed a place in heaven. The granting of indulgences was contingent on a hefty donation.

In addition to making calls for the end of corrupt practices, some church activists (who were not part of the higher reaches of the church's structure) began to question certain religious practices. One specific issue concerned the church's teaching that only priests could be conduits between people and God. The religious activists asserted that this was not necessary. Instead, they said, anyone could have a direct relationship with God. By the early 1500s, during the Renaissance, this dissent grew so strong that it created one of the defining moments of the era, a movement called the Reformation. The Reformation split the church and divided it into two factions, the Protestant and Roman Catholic faiths.

For centuries afterwards, this split created hostility, political intrigue, and sometimes open warfare. Among the many examples of conflict caused by religious differences during this period was the Thirty Years' War, a series of bloody clashes in what is now Germany. It pitted Catholics and Protestants from many nations against each other in a bid for political power and religious dominance. Although tension between these two factions has more or less faded away since then, remnants of it can still be seen in the world today.

Coluj potej che dal suo difuj
fu trãsmutato damo in baccbigliõe
doue lascio limal protesi neruj

Di piu duej mal uedre el simone
piu logo esser nõ puo pchio ueggio
la surger nuouo fummo del sabione

Gente uiẽ colaquale ess̃ nõ ueggio
siete ricõmãdato el mio tesoro
nei quale io uiuo ancora e piu nõ cheggio

Poi si ruolse e parue di coloro
che corono auerona el drapo uerde
per lacipagna e parue di costoro

Quelli che uince nõ coluj che perde

The religious and romantic themes of the fourteenth-century Italian writer Dante Alighieri influenced many later poets. A manuscript page illustrates a scene from Dante's epic poem, The Divine Comedy. In this scene, sinners wander naked within fortress walls burning with everlasting flames.

Influences Abound

In addition to the changes in religion that began in the late Middle Ages, the era's scholarly and artistic advances similarly left a deep legacy for future historical eras. In particular the flowering of education, art, literature, architecture, theater, technological invention, and exploration during the Renaissance all had their roots in the late Middle Ages. One prominent example was the increasing sophistication of architecture. The development of the soaring Gothic churches of the late Middle Ages, with their high, strong arches and flying buttresses to support walls, paved the way for further advances during the Renaissance (although Renaissance architecture was also influenced by other styles). Another example was the work of the fourteenth-century Italian writer Dante Alighieri. Dante's religious and romantic themes, as well as his strong and unadorned style, powerfully influenced many later important poets including William Shakespeare, Edmund Spenser, and John Milton.

The late Middle Ages, in short, paved the way for the dramatic surge of culture and technology that would take place during the Renaissance. The Renaissance was a period of tremendous intellectual exploration, as well as the exploration of new lands, for the nations of Europe. But that exploration would not have happened in the way it did if it had not been for the events of the late Middle Ages. J.M. Roberts writes, "It becomes clear that [the centuries of the late Middle Ages were] opening the way to something quite different. An age of adventure and revolution was under way."[35]

No specific event or absolute date separates the late Middle Ages from the Renaissance. The transition was a gradual process over many years—a transition that involved the change from a religious society that emphasized the community to a secular society that highlighted the individual. Although historians often disagree over the approximate time the Middle Ages gave rise to the Renaissance, consensus seems to favor the middle of the fifteenth century.

No matter what end point is chosen, however, one thing is clear. The late Middle Ages remains one of the most innovative and influential periods in world and European history.

Source Notes

Introduction: The Defining Characteristics of the Late Middle Ages

1. J.M. Roberts, *A History of Europe*. New York: Allen Lane/Penguin, 1996, p. 123.
2. Stu Witmer, e-mail to author, October 15, 2010.

Chapter One: What Events Led to the Late Middle Ages?

3. C. Warren Hollister, *Medieval Europe: A Short History*. Boston: McGraw-Hill, 1998, p. 146.
4. Colin McEvedy, *The New Penguin Atlas of Medieval History*. New York: Penguin, 1992, p. 44.

Chapter Two: Redefining Nations

5. Roberts, *A History of Europe*, p. 106.
6. Dana Carlton Munro, ed., "Documents Illustrative of Feudalism," in *Translations and Reprints from the Original Sources of European History*, vol. 4, no. 3. Philadelphia: Department of History of the University of Pennsylvania, 1902, pp. 2–32.
7. Roberts, *A History of Europe*, p. 173.
8. Norman F. Cantor, *The Civilization of the Middle Ages*. New York: HarperCollins, 1993, pp. 238–39.
9. Jennifer Meagher, "The Holy Roman Empire and the Habsburgs, 1400–1600," Heilbrunn Timeline of Art History, Metropolitan Museum of Art, 2000–2011. www.metmuseum.org.
10. "Tu Felix Austria Nube," The World of the Habsburgs, 2010. http://english.habsburger.net.
11. L. Kip Wheeler, "The Hundred Years' War," Carson-Newman College, 1998–2011. http://web.cn.edu/kwheeler.
12. McEvedy, *The New Penguin Atlas of Medieval History*, p. 8.

Chapter Three: Religion and the Church

13. Quoted in Barbara H. Rosenwein, *A Short History of the Middle Ages*. Toronto, ON: Broadview, 2002, p. 120.

14. McEvedy, *The New Penguin Atlas of Medieval History*, p. 72.

15. Roberts, *A History of Europe*, p. 164.

16. Quoted in Susan Wise Bauer, *The History of the Medieval World: From the Conversion of Constantine to the First Crusade*. New York: Norton, 2010, p. 654.

17. Cantor, *The Civilization of the Middle Ages*, p. 292.

18. Quoted in Frances Gies, *The Knight in History*. New York: Harper & Row, 1984, p. 45.

19. Quoted in Hollister, *Medieval Europe*, p. 198.

20. Quoted in Hollister, *Medieval Europe*, p. 245.

21. Roberts, *A History of Europe*, p. 169.

22. McEvedy, *The New Penguin Atlas of Medieval History*, p. 100.

Chapter Four: Feudalism, the Medieval Economy, and Society

23. Jacques Le Goff, ed., *Medieval Callings*. Chicago: University of Chicago Press, 1990, p. 34.

24. Will Durant and Ariel Durant, *The Story of Civilization:* Vol. 4: *The Age of Faith*. New York: Simon & Schuster, 1980, p. 620.

25. Hollister, *Medieval Europe*, p. 172.

26. McEvedy, *The New Penguin Atlas of Medieval History*, p. 74.

27. Hollister, *Medieval Europe*, p. 156.

28. Quoted in "The Black Death: Bubonic Plague," The Middle Ages.net, 2010. www.themiddleages.net.

29. Le Goff, *Medieval Callings*, p. 35.

30. Quoted in Nigel Saul, ed., *The Oxford Illustrated History of Medieval England*. Oxford: Oxford University Press, 1997, p. 102.

31. Quoted in "Innocent III (1198–1216) and the Fourth Lateran Council (1215)," US Naval Academy. http://usna.edu.

32. Roberts, *A History of Europe*, p. 160.

Chapter Five: What Is the Legacy of the Late Middle Ages?

33. Geoffrey Barraclough, *The Crucible of Europe*. Berkeley: University of California Press, 1976, p. 9.

34. Quoted in Peter Haidu, *The Subject Medieval/Modern: Text and Governance in the Middle Ages*. Palo Alto, CA: Stanford University Press, 1993, p. 1.

35. Roberts, *A History of Europe*, p. 163.

Important People of the Late Middle Ages

Alexius I, John II, and Manuel I: Rulers of the Comnenus dynasty of the Byzantine Empire, who had close relationships with the European crusaders and did much to restore (for a time) the empire's power and influence to a level it had enjoyed during the early Middle Ages.

Clement V: The first of the popes during the Avignon papacy, when rivals to popes in Rome governed the church from the city of Avignon.

Gregory VII: One of the popes who called for major reforms of the church in the late Middle Ages.

Henry IV: A king of Germany who rebelled against Gregory VII's attempts at reform.

Joan of Arc: The brave French peasant girl who became a leader in the Hundred Years' War against the English.

John I: The English king who was forced to sign the Magna Carta, a key document in the rise of representative government and civil law.

Louis VI of France: The most influential of the Capetian line of French rulers. The Capetians were largely responsible for France's rise to power in Europe during the late Middle Ages.

Richard II: The English king at the time of Wat Tyler's Rebellion, an important moment in the decline of feudalism.

Urban II: The pope who called for the First Crusade against Muslim forces in Jerusalem.

William the Conqueror (William I): The leader of the Norman Conquest that captured England and helped make it a permanently unified nation.

For Further Research

Books

Norman Bancroft-Hunt, *Living in the Middle Ages*. New York: Chelsea House, 2008.

Kevin Cunningham, *Bubonic Plague*. Edina, MN: Essential Library, 2011.

Stephen Currie, *Medieval Crusades*. San Diego, CA: Lucent, 2009.

Peter Edwards, *Europe and the Middle Ages*. Upper Saddle River, NJ: Prentice Hall, 2009.

Katherine Hinds, *Everyday Life in Medieval Europe*. Tarrytown, NY: Marshall Cavendish, 2008.

Laura Scandiffio, *Crusades: Kids at the Crossroads*. Toronto, ON: Annick, 2009.

Pamela White, *Exploration in the World of the Middle Ages, 500–1500*. New York: Chelsea House, 2009.

Websites

"The Bayeux Tapestry" (www.hastings1066.com/baythumb.shtml). This site provides information on and full-color photographs of the famous tapestry commemorating the Battle of Hastings.

"Castles on the Web" (www.castlesontheweb.com/). As the name implies, this site has extensive information, photos, and more focused on the castles of medieval Europe.

"The European Middle Ages" (www.wsu.edu:8080/%7Edee/MA/MA.HTM). This site, maintained by a history professor at Washington State University's history department, has extensive essays on a wide range of topics.

"Medieval Age 1066–1500," Learn History (www.learnhistory.org.uk/medieval). This site focuses on British history but has many good articles on the Middle Ages.

"Medieval Art Museum Collections Online," New York Carver.com (www.newyorkcarver.com/museum.htm). This site is not specifically for young readers, but it has links to wonderful reproductions of medieval art from museums all over the world.

"Medieval Life and Times" (www.medieval-life-and-times.info/). This site has concise articles on many topics covering the Middle Ages.

The Middle Ages.net (www.themiddleages.net). A site with excellent articles and many links to other sites on the subject of the Middle Ages.

Index

Picture Credits

About the Author

Adam Woog has written many books for adults, young adults, and children. He has a special interest in history and wrote *The Early Middle Ages*. Woog lives with his wife in Seattle, Washington, and they have a daughter in college.